Joanna
McClelland
Glass

Toronto
4/28/05

TRYING

TRYING

Joanna McClelland Glass

Playwrights Canada Press
Toronto • Canada

Playwrights Canada Press
215 Spadina Ave. Toronto, Ontario CANADA M5T 2C7
416.703.0013   fax 416.408.3402
orders@playwrightscanada.com • www.playwrightscanada.com

Playwrights Canada Press acknowledges the financial support of the
Canadian taxpayer through the Government of Canada Book Publishing
Industry Development Programme (BPIDP) for our publishing activities.
We also acknowledge the Canadian and Ontario taxpayers through the
Canada Council for the Arts and the Ontario Arts Council.

The Canada Council for the Arts
Le Conseil des Arts du Canada

ONTARIO ARTS COUNCIL
CONSEIL DES ARTS DE L'ONTARIO

Cover photo: "Light in the Forest" by Freeman Patterson
Cover design: JLArt
Production Editor: MZK

Library and Archives Canada Cataloguing in Publication

Glass, Joanna M.
    Trying / Joanna McClelland Glass.

A play.
ISBN 0-88754-812-1

    I. Title.

PS8563.L369T79 2005   C812'.54   C2005-902002-4

First edition: May 2005.
Printed and bound by Printco at Toronto, Canada.

In memory of George Sperdakos

Our thanks to Liveright Publishing Corporation for the use of the excerpts from e.e. cummings poetry

The Kew garden quote on page 77 is taken from Alfred Noyes' "The Barrel Organ"

Trying was originally produced at Victory Gardens Theater, Chicago, Illinois, March 29, 2004, with the following company:

Judge Frances Biddle	Fritz Weaver
Sarah Schorr	Kati Brazda
Artistic Director	Dennis Zacek
Production Director	Sandy Shinner
Stage Manager	Tina M. Jach
Set Designer	Jeff Bauer
Lighting	Jacqueline Reid
Costumes	Carolyn Cristofani
Sound	Andrew Hopson

•••

Trying was originally produced on the New York Stage by Michael Leavitt Maidstone Productions, October 14, 2004, Libby Adler Mages, Mari Stuart, Tony D'Angelo, Steve Dahl, Maria Cozzi, Sandy Shinner, Production Director.

•••

It was also produced at The Promenade Theatre, New York City, in October 2004 with the following company:

Judge Frances Biddle	Fritz Weaver
Sarah Schorr	Kati Brazda
Artistic Director	Dennis Zacek
Director	Sandy Shinner
Stage Manager	Andrea Testani
Set Designer	Jeff Bauer
Lighting	Jacqueline Reid
Costumes	Carolyn Cristofani
Sound	Andrew Hopson

•••

Trying had its Canadian premiere September 16, 2004 at the National Arts Centre, Ottawa; Marti Maraden, Artistic Director. Co-Produced with the Canadian Stage Company; Martin Bragg, Artistic Producer – with the following company:

Judge Francis Biddle	Paul Soles
Sarah Schorr	Caroline Cave
Director	Marti Maraden
Stage Manager	Laurie Champagne
Set and Costume Design	Christina Poddubiuk
Lighting	John (Jock) Munro
Sound	Peter McBoyle

SET

The play is set in Georgetown, Washington, D.C. It is November of 1967.

The set is an office that is located over a double garage. The garage was once a stable. (The distance that Biddle must navigate, between the house and the garage, is approximately one hundred and fifty feet.) In order to enter the office one must climb the stairs within the garage.

The entrance is at stage right. Nearby there is a free-standing antique bentwood hanger. The back wall is full of old, legal-type, glass-fronted book cabinets. There are also built-in wall book-shelves. These house books, magazines, scrapbooks that have been collected over sixty years. Somewhere along the back wall there is a door to a bathroom. There could be, at stage left, a window. There are several old filing cabinets and a couple of tables. The surfaces of these are covered with yellowed files and journals. There is a not-immediately noticeable "coffee" table that has a sugar bowl on it. There is a free-standing globe and a lectern-type stand that holds a dictionary. There is a cot that Biddle relies on for naps. There are a couple of threadbare oriental rugs, discarded from the house, on the floor. Behind Biddle's desk there are auto-graphed photographs of famous Democratic politicians from the nineteen thirties, forties and fifties.

Sarah's desk is at stage right; Biddle's ancient, rather battered desk at stage left. Ideally there should only be about fifteen feet between the desks. Biddle sits in a swivel chair that has arms. There is, in front of his desk, an armless "secretary's chair."Each desk has a phone on it. The line to and from the house "buzzes," the outside line rings.

The office is heated by two old metal gas heaters, one at stage left, one at stage right. They are approximately two feet wide by four feet high. The dials that control them are low on their sides, near the floor. Either there is a chair near each heater, or Biddle drags a chair to each so that he can help himself up and down when adjusting the dials.

CHARACTERS

JUDGE BIDDLE:

An eighty-one-year-old, once brilliant man who was Attorney General of the United States under Franklin Roosevelt. After a long and illustrious career he now functions, as he says, "somewhere between lucidity and senility."He is the aristocratic scion of an old, Main Line Philadelphia family.

SARAH SCHORR:

A twenty-five-year-old girl who has been hired, by Mrs. Biddle, to be the Judge's secretary. She is a direct, plain-spoken, pleasant girl, originally from the prairie province of Saskatchewan.

PLAYWRIGHT'S NOTE

In the 1967-68, pre-computer years, carbon copies were made of all correspondence. Filing the copies would be an activity for Sarah.

SCENE ONE

It is the second week of November, 1967. It is eight-thirty-five on a Monday morning.

As the lights come up we see SARAH, seated in the "secretary's chair" in front of JUDGE BIDDLE'S desk. She wears a hat, scarf, winter coat, gloves, and has a shoulder bag. She is trying not to shiver. She has been alone in the cold, unfamiliar, unheated room for five minutes. She has, prior to the opening of the play, placed a small tray containing a thermos bottle and two china mugs on a filing cabinet. She has also placed a bundle of mail on the "secretary's" desk. It is in a small canvas sack with handles.

Simultaneously, as the lights come up, we hear a door close downstairs. JUDGE BIDDLE begins his climb up the stairs from the garage. There are fourteen stairs. He has a metal pin in his left ankle and that foot drags. We hear the strong thud of the right foot on a stair, followed by a dragging up of the left foot. These are two distinct sounds. When he finally enters the room he is wearing a hat, ear-muffs, a long scarf, gloves and a heavy coat. He wears wet low-cut black "rubbers" over his shoes.

It is a given that BIDDLE's various ailments keep him in almost constant discomfort.

BIDDLE   Good morning.

SARAH   Good morning.

He moves to the bentwood coat hanger near the door. He removes his hat and hangs it up. The removal of the other outer clothing is slow and laborious because his arthritic hands barely function. By the time he says, "Did you meet the house staff?", the removals are complete. He wears a tweed jacket, shirt and tie, and heavy wool pants.

BIDDLE   It's "Sarah," isn't it?

SARAH   Yes, sir.

BIDDLE   Sarah with an "h"?

SARAH   Yes, sir.

BIDDLE   Mrs. Sarah Schorr.

SARAH   Yes, sir. My husband recently—

BIDDLE   How long have you been married?

SARAH   Two years.

BIDDLE   You're twenty-five years old?

SARAH   Yes, sir.

BIDDLE   And you're Canadian.

SARAH   Yes, sir.

BIDDLE   My wife and I have found that Canadians, quite consistently, are dependably civil. Do you like living in D.C.?

SARAH   We've only been here four months. My husband received his doctorate in June.

BIDDLE   In what, and where?

SARAH   In Economics. At Yale.

BIDDLE   My father went to Yale, but I'm a Harvard man myself. We used to say, "Harvard was old Harvard, when Yale was still a pup." What's your husband's name?

SARAH Paul. He came to D.C. to work for—

BIDDLE Sarah-with-an-h, you might as well know that I have very little interest in the husbands. Over the years, I've been obliged to listen to a surfeit of secretarial matrimonial sagas, and I no longer have the resources for it.

> *Brief pause.*

Were you at Smith?

SARAH No, sir.

BIDDLE Radcliffe? Wellesley?

SARAH No, sir, I'm not one of those.

BIDDLE One of those what?

SARAH One of the pleated-plaid Ivy girls.

> *He detects the "edge" in her answer and looks at her for a moment.*

BIDDLE Ah. Katherine told me that but I'd forgotten. I'm sorry I wasn't able to interview you personally. I was bedridden that day.

SARAH Yes, Mrs. Biddle explained that you were ill.

BIDDLE I'm always ill. I am ill unrelievedly. I've got a list of ailments from here to Mt. Rushmore. Occasionally I'm ill horizontally, but mostly I'm ill vertically. Katherine liked you very much.

SARAH   Thank you. I sensed that at the interview. But I was quite surprised when she phoned last week.

BIDDLE   Were you? Why?

SARAH   Well, she had implied, very politely of course, that I might be too young. She said that, generally, you preferred older, more matronly women.

BIDDLE   That has been my preference. Because where I am is where they'd soon be. So one could hope for empathy. I tried to hire retired civil servants. The last one, however, was an unmitigated disaster. Stupid in the extreme. I had to let her go. Whereupon Katherine persuaded me to make an exception. "Find someone young," she said. "Young and pliable."

               Brief pause.

               Your previous employment was with an advertising agency?

SARAH   Yes, sir.

BIDDLE   What did you do there?

SARAH   I was a copywriter.

               He sits to remove his rubbers.

BIDDLE   Do you mean that awful blather is actually composed by somebody?

SARAH   Yes, sir. I hope, at some time in the future, to write more seriously.

BIDDLE   Do you know what's wrong with, "Winston tastes good like a cigarette should."?

SARAH   Yes, sir. It should be "as" a cigarette should.

BIDDLE   Indeed it should. Our language is deteriorating at the speed of light. May I ask why you didn't apply to an ad agency in D.C.?

SARAH   Well, now that my husband's finished school, I can take a part-time job. And this position looked very interesting.

BIDDLE   I see.

                Placing the wet rubbers.

              This snow two weeks before Thanksgiving is most unusual. To my amazement Pierre got out early and shovelled a path across the yard. Did you meet the house staff?

SARAH   Yes, I came through the kitchen on my way over.

BIDDLE   They're a man and wife team. French. They came to us via William Bullitt. Bill Bullitt was the first American ambassador to the Soviet Union. Monique cooks, Pierre butles and is man-Friday.

SARAH   Monique asked me to bring the thermos tray.

                He looks at the "coffee table" and sees nothing.

BIDDLE   Where did you put it?

SARAH   Over there, on the file cabinet.

BIDDLE   No. We put the tray—we put the tray—

                He pauses, losing his train of thought.

              The tray and the mail have to be lugged by the secretary. It's difficult for me to climb stairs and carry things. I've got a metal pin in my ankle. Did you bring the mail?

SARAH   Yes, I did.

> *He has now removed all of his outerwear. He shuffles over to the first heater.*

BIDDLE   It's idiotic, at my age, keeping my office over the garage. Especially since I have to limp across the yard to get here. But houses tend to be seats of domesticity. I learned, very early on, that cerebral efforts haven't a hope in hell in the midst of the women and the ladies. Although I guess that distinction—the women and the ladies—is outmoded now.

> *SARAH hides a shiver and he scowls.*

Obviously, you're cold.

SARAH   Yes, a little.

BIDDLE   You're cold because you came early, and not when you were told to come. You probably wanted to make a good impression on your first day. You'll find, if you stay, that I'm far more impressed by adherence to rules.

SARAH   I'm sorry. I did want—

BIDDLE   The place is heated by these hideous gas heaters. The operation of them—this is very important—the operation of them must be left entirely to me. We will work mornings only, nine until noon. If I arrive at eight-thirty, and you arrive at nine, I'll have the heaters up and running.

> *He sighs, wishing that he was not "obliged" to say the following.*

And I suppose I must add, since employers are obliged to set terms, that if you arrive at nine-fifteen you'll be tardy and I'll be irritable. Now.

> *He must bend down to the dial near the floor. As he bends, he leans on the nearby chair. There is pain in the bend and pain in his hand as he turns the dial.*

These damned heaters are as ancient as I am. The imbecile who designed them put the dials down at the floor. I should get something with a wall dial, but I won't go to the expense because I don't expect to last much longer. In fact, I'm fairly certain this is my final year.

> *He can not rise without clutching the chair. He then eyes the far heater, stage left. He starts his shuffle.*

That's the bathroom, over there. If you're like all the others, you'll go in there to cry.

SARAH   *(assertively)* Perhaps I won't be like all the others.

BIDDLE   The odds are against it.

> *When he arrives at the second heater he leans on the nearby chair and bends. SARAH finds this arduous routine difficult to witness.*

SARAH   Please, Judge Biddle, may I help you—

BIDDLE   You may not! You must never, ever, touch the heaters. Not at nine, not at noon, never. Five years ago the secretary thought she'd turned them off when she left, but in fact she'd turned them to high, and she set the place on fire. There. It'll warm up soon.

> *Rising from the floor.*

Katherine sang your praises most insistently.

SARAH   Thank you. How is Mrs. Biddle's arthritis today?

BIDDLE　　She's got the heating pad on it. Did she interview you in the study?

SARAH　　No, we had tea in the living room. The house is very old, isn't it?

BIDDLE　　Not for Georgetown. Eighteen thirty. This building used to be a stable and this, of course, was the hayloft.

SARAH　　*(She is at once shy and enthusiastic.)* I was absolutely stunned at your Cezanne. I mean, to walk into a private home and see a Cezanne just—hanging there.

BIDDLE　　It's been in the family for years. My branch of the Philadelphia Biddles were avid collectors. I gather that, since you know your Cezanne from your Gauguin, you appreciate art?

SARAH　　Yes, I do.

　　　　　　　He begins his shuffle toward his desk.

BIDDLE　　And literature?

SARAH　　Poetry, mostly.

BIDDLE　　Really?

SARAH　　Yes. I read voraciously.

BIDDLE　　That usage of that adverb is a thorn in my side. Webster disagrees with me, but I'm old enough to say to hell with Webster. I prefer it that one eats voraciously, but reads voluminously. Reads volumes extensively. Please don't employ that usage again.

SARAH　　No, sir, I won't.

BIDDLE   It's a thorn in my side. Did Katherine tell you that she's a published poet?

SARAH   No, sir.

BIDDLE   Well, she's modest. I would have had a very narrow, very restricted legal life had it not been for Katherine and her artistic friends.

>   *Pause.*

I suppose she told you that I'm "difficult"?

SARAH   *(a little too brightly)* No, sir, not exactly.

BIDDLE   Did she say the job would require a certain... fortitude?

SARAH   Not... exactly.

BIDDLE   Oh, come now, she must have at least implied that your sojourn here would not be a bed of roses.

SARAH   Well, actually, yes, she implied... words to that effect.

BIDDLE   Of course she did. I know her. What did she say was the primary prerequisite for the job?

SARAH   *(brief pause)* She said, "spine."

BIDDLE   Ah. Spine.

>   *In conclusion.*

Well, she hired you, so I will deduce that you have that.

SARAH   Yes, sir, I think I can summon it when I need it.

BIDDLE   We shall see. Now, where were we? Oh, yes, the
           heaters. You see, she swore she'd turned them off, but
           in fact she left them on high. Up in ashes. Historically
           significant papers from my years as A. G. Attorney
           General. I was A.G. under Roosevelt, 1941 to 1945.
           My maternal great-great grandfather was the first
           Attorney General. Edmund Randolph of Virginia.
           Appointed by George Washington.

                    He stops at the "coffee table" and glares at it
                    lengthily.

           This is not good. The thermos tray is not on the coffee
           table. For some mysterious reason the thermos tray is
           on the filing cabinet.

SARAH   Sir, I just—

BIDDLE   It doesn't belong on the filing cabinet. It belongs on
           the table with the sugar bowl. I told you that a minute
           ago.

SARAH   No, sir, you didn't.

BIDDLE   I'm certain I did.

SARAH   Perhaps you—intended to.

BIDDLE   If I didn't, your powers of observation should have
           informed you. How absolutely perverse to see a sugar
           bowl and then set the thermos on the filing cabinet.
           Forgive me for observing that your powers of obser-
           vation leave a great deal to be desired.

                    SARAH, astounded at his bluntness, retrieves the
                    thermos tray and places it properly.

SARAH   I'm sorry.

He reaches his desk but does not sit down. He grimaces.

BIDDLE   Damn! My intestines are at war with the rest of me.

He sits down.

Up in ashes. My entire collection of Daumier lithographs. No one caricatured the legal profession quite like Daumier. And two of my private journals from the Nuremberg Trials. I was Chief American Judge of the International Military Tribunal at Nuremberg in 1946. Appointed, of course, by Truman. You'll see that much of what was left is scorched. Oftentimes, when I refer to an old book, I can still smell the smoke.

He pauses,"tuning out," gazing into space, remembering the fire sirens.

And hear the sirens.

SARAH waits a moment.

SARAH   (*gently*) Judge Biddle, Mrs. Biddle said you would outline my duties.

BIDDLE   I'd like a cup of coffee, please. Unless, of course, you consider that task altogether too menial in this year of our Lord, 1967. What with Betty Friedan, and half of you out there burning your—

He is suddenly embarrassed.

Your upper underwear.

SARAH   I'm happy to get it.

BIDDLE   I'm sure you're not happy, but we'll deal with that when it surfaces. *If you stay.*

SARAH   Sir, it's my intention to stay. Why would I not?

BIDDLE   I will be eighty-two next year. You will find that I'm old and ailing and cranky. You will find that I function, when I function at all, somewhere between lucidity and senility. I'm set in my ways. And Katherine insists that I'm guilty of the regrettable habit of always having to have the last word.

> *Pause.*

Did you tell me your age?

SARAH   Twenty-five.

BIDDLE   Two lumps of sugar, please, and help yourself. I was fifty-six when you were born. If I were you I wouldn't be quite so confident of your staying powers. We can't help but find each other extremely trying.

SARAH   I made a promise. I promised Mrs. Biddle that I'd try.

BIDDLE   Try?

SARAH   Yes.

BIDDLE   *(sarcastically)* Well, isn't that admirable. God knows I need help. Look at this desk. Paper chaos. It's absolutely crushing.

SARAH   *(delivering the coffee)* Should I set this here?

BIDDLE   No, over there. Thank you.

SARAH   You're welcome. Sir, Mrs. Biddle said that you'd outline my duties.

> *A moment passes as he surveys his desk.*

BIDDLE   It would seem, quite unaccountably, that the mail has piss-a-deared. Where is the mail?

SARAH   I put it over there, on the secretary's desk.

BIDDLE   Well, that is not good. Really, your placement of things is decidedly irregular. Explain to me why my mail is on the secretary's desk?

SARAH   I assumed that you'd want me to open it.

BIDDLE   I don't. Do you see this letter opener? *(holding up a silver opener)* Henry James visited Philadelphia and gave this to my mother in nineteen-oh-five. It has not become, as I have, obsolete. Fetch my mail, please, from the secretary's desk.

> *SARAH gets the mail. She carries it to BIDDLE's desk. He squints at her.*

And I wish you'd shed that coat. You look like Peary at the North Pole.

> *SARAH goes to the hanger and removes her coat, etc. BIDDLE watches a moment and waits.*

May I deduce, from your movement, that you heard me?

SARAH   Yes, sir.

BIDDLE   Well, then, respond!

SARAH   Yes, sir.

> *He opens the mail sack and removes a handful of mail.*

BIDDLE   You moderns are bereft of all social grace. I call you feeble moderns. *(to himself)* Or is it feckless moderns? No matter. Both apply.

> *He lifts an opened letter that's been on his desk for weeks.*

This is from Jacob Pearlman, historian at Princeton. Professor Pearlman wants to know if Felix Frankfurter suggested me for Solicitor General. I was Solicitor General before I was Attorney General. The short answer is yes.

> *Holding up another letter.*

This is from a publisher in New York who is waiting for my memoirs. He dares to remind me that he has a contract. That I am several chapters in arrears. You type, of course?

SARAH   Yes, sir.

BIDDLE   And you have shorthand?

SARAH   Yes, sir.

BIDDLE   Gregg, hopefully?

SARAH   No, it's called Speedwriting.

BIDDLE   Speedwriting? Does that mean something, or is it just modern babble? Does it mean that you write English speedily, as I speak it?

SARAH   Yes, it's a combination of symbols and letters.

BIDDLE   Alphabetical letters?

SARAH   Yes. And symbols.

BIDDLE   Show me. Go fetch a pad.

> *SARAH goes to the secretary's desk, finding a pad and pen.*

I don't understand why, if you're going to go to the bother of learning chicken-scratch, why you don't learn the time-honored Gregg. Take this down, please. "When the elite meet to eat, the talk is refined." Let me see it.

> *She passes her steno pad across his desk.*

Well, isn't that peculiar?

SARAH   It's what's being taught nowadays.

BIDDLE   *(baiting her)* And therefore you consider it better?

SARAH   Not necessarily.

> *Again, he tunes out, gazing into space, frowning.*

BIDDLE   What was her name?

SARAH   Who, sir?

BIDDLE   The one who had Pittman, rather than Gregg.

SARAH   I don't know, sir.

BIDDLE   It was a flower name. Help me.

> *She thinks, then tries.*

SARAH   Mmmm. Rose?

BIDDLE   No.

SARAH   *(thinking)* Iris?

BIDDLE No. Mormon girl. The Mormons like the flowery names.

SARAH Lily? Violet?

BIDDLE Marigold! She learned Pittman instead of Gregg.

He gazes off, remembering Marigold.

Marigold the Mormon.

SARAH *(interrupting his reverie)* Sir? Perhaps now would be a good time to outline my duties.

BIDDLE God-a-mighty, you sound like a broken record! Do you think I find these initiation mornings easy? It's all very easy for you, at twenty-five, breezing in here both eager and early. But can you even imagine how stressful the hiring process is for an old man? Calling employment agencies, interviewing, getting references? Having to trot out a welcome-wagon full of appropriate noises for the thousandth time?

SARAH *(after a moment)* Sir, Mrs. Biddle explained that this morning would be stressful for you. I didn't arrive expecting appropriate noises. But I would very much appreciate some instruction as to my duties.

BIDDLE Madam, you are nothing if not single-minded.

The "house" phone buzzes. BIDDLE reaches for the receiver. His right hand throbs with pain.
He barks:

Yes?

Katherine says: "I know you can't talk."

Katherine, if you know I can't talk, why are you calling?

Katherine wonders how it's going.

How do you think it's going? It's going very badly.

She asks if he's behaving himself.

No, I'm not behaving myself. It'll be a miracle, an absolute four-star-fish-and-loaves-miracle if she stays.

He bangs down the receiver.

I am quite undone. I've got floaters in my vision. Your nagging has quite undone me.

He rises, in pain.

I need to stretch out. I have to lie down on the cot.

As he moves to the cot.

You'll see, over there on your desk, a pile of bills.

SARAH moves to her desk.

The household chequebook hasn't been reconciled in months. Apparently I paid last month's phone bill three times, and didn't pay the light bill at all. And I'm receiving rude letters from the water company. Go and reconcile the chequebook.

SARAH   Yes, sir.

> *He is now inert on the cot. SARAH sits at her desk. It is a foreign place and she must look for the chequebook.*
>
> *There is a long pause. BIDDLE is so without movement that SARAH becomes concerned. She whispers:*

SARAH   Judge Biddle?

    There is no reaction. She is afraid that he has died.

  (quietly, but alarmed) Judge Biddle?

    BIDDLE reaches down, with difficulty, and pulls
    up an "afghan," to cover him.

BIDDLE   Your duties will include many a foray to the Post
    Office. A large percentage of the population is writing
    books about Franklin Delano Roosevelt. They write
    voluminously and then they pack it off to me for veri-
    fication. It's bad enough that I have to read it and it's
    worse that I have to muck about with returning it.
    May I assume that, if you don't find pouring coffee
    too menial, you won't mind running errands?

SARAH   No, sir, I won't mind.

BIDDLE   If I fall asleep and noon creeps around, leave quietly
    and do not touch the heaters.

SARAH   Yes, sir.

BIDDLE   And take the thermos tray, and the mail sack back to
    the house.

SARAH   Yes, sir. Sir, do you have the cancelled cheques?

BIDDLE   Did you hear me? I said do not touch the heaters.

SARAH   I will not touch the heaters.

    SARAH moves a sheet of paper in front of her, to
    try and address the chequebook's mathematics.

BIDDLE   Not at nine, not at noon, never. She knew very well that all the way right was all the way on, and all the way left was all the way off. Droit, gauche. Simple enough but she couldn't get it through her thick skull.

        The lights fade.

        Blackout.

ACT ONE

SCENE TWO

The following day, Tuesday. It is 9:00 A.M. The hanger remains draped with BIDDLE's winter garb. He now wears a cardigan sweater with shirt and tie. He sits at his desk, upset. He picks up the "house" phone and buzzes.

BIDDLE   Katherine, I can not let this morning pass without saying that your comments at breakfast wounded me.

    Pause.

That's not true.

    Pause.

That is not why I'm calling.

    Pause.

I do not always have to have the last word!

    We hear the downstairs door close. SARAH runs up the garage stairs.

Here she comes. We'll have to discuss it later.

    He puts the receiver down. SARAH enters, carrying the thermos tray. The "mail sack" is looped over her wrist. She takes the tray to the coffee table and then delivers the sack to BIDDLE's desk.

SARAH   Good morning.

BIDDLE   Good morning. It's precisely 9:00 A.M., and that is good.

SARAH   Thank you.

BIDDLE   I have the heat up and running.

SARAH   Yes, I can feel it.

BIDDLE   I'm sorry I conked out on you yesterday. First days,
          with a new one, are rather like a dreaded exam.

SARAH   Yes, sir, I understand. Here is your mail, and—
          (handing him a note) Monique asked me to give you
          this note.

BIDDLE   We don't call Monique Monique. We call Monique
          "Cook".

SARAH   Really?

BIDDLE   Yes. That is our habit.

          *He puts the note aside and opens the mail sack. He
          takes out a handful of mail.*

          I've had a terrific tune-up with my wife this morning,
          and it's left me unravelled. *(suspiciously)* Or has she
          reported that to you already, since you're such pals?

          *SARAH removes her coat and hat at the bentwood
          hanger.*

SARAH   No, sir.

BIDDLE   Are you sure? Not—conspiratorily in the back hall?

SARAH   Sir, I haven't seen Mrs. Biddle this morning.

BIDDLE   She was downright surly at breakfast. She said she
           knew instinctively, after only one day, that I wasn't
           trying to make our association work. And I took
           umbrage. I resent the implication that something,
           anything, is expected of me in my final year.

                   Brief pause.

           It's inconceivable to me that these truths are not self-
           evident. I'm in the process of leaving this life. The exit
           sign is flashing over the door and the door is ajar. You
           would think a spouse of fifty years would know that.
           God, I hate tune-ups! They hang over the day like
           a shroud. And then they hover over dinner and sully
           every mouthful.

                   Brief pause.

           By the way, I forgot to tell you, that's the bathroom
           over there.

SARAH   Yes, thank you. *(gently)* May I get you a cup of coffee?

BIDDLE   When I want it, I'll ask for it.

                   *He gestures at the "secretary's chair," in front of his
                   desk.*

           Come and sit down.

                   She sits in front of his desk.

           Did you reconcile the chequebook?

SARAH   I'm afraid that's going to take more time.

                   Embarrassed, she proceeds cautiously.

           You see, it's not just a case of paying the same bill
           three times, it's a case of... well, sir, unfortunately, it's

a case of paying the same bill three times with differing amounts. And then deducting the differing amounts three times. That's why, when the statement arrives, you have much, much more in the bank than you do in the chequebook.

BIDDLE   Madam, you are bold.

SARAH   I'm sorry.

BIDDLE   You are not discreet.

SARAH   Sir, I was just trying to illustrate the extent of the problem.

BIDDLE   Once upon a time I had a mind like a steel trap.

> *Brief pause.*

Can you fix it?

SARAH   Yes, sir, I can. In time.

BIDDLE   *(lifting a letter from the mail)* Look at this "In" basket. Overflowing. And this letter from the publisher is dated mid-September. And here we are with Thanksgiving right around the corner. I just can't face it. I may have to lie down.

SARAH   Judge Biddle, please, don't despair. Let's make a stab at it.

BIDDLE   I can't.

> *Pause.*

It's the tune-up at breakfast.

SARAH   Please, sir, try and rally.

BIDDLE   I can't rally.

Thinking of his promise to Katherine.

But I suppose I have to try. Before I do, perhaps you could tell me, where are you from, in Canada?

SARAH   Saskatchewan.

BIDDLE   *(rising)* Come show me.

He shuffles over to the globe. SARAH follows.

It's that big rectangle in the middle, isn't it?

SARAH   Yes, it's one of the western provinces.

Turning the globe.

There. Saskatoon, Saskatchewan.

BIDDLE   Dear me. It's very far away from everything.

SARAH   Yes.

BIDDLE   I mean, it's not even near Chicago. Ten provinces?

SARAH   Yes, sir.

BIDDLE   And you have "Premiers" rather than Governors.

SARAH   Yes. Our most famous one, in Saskatchewan, is Tommy Douglas. He's the man who pioneered Canada's universal health plan.

BIDDLE   Really? Tell me about Tommy Douglas.

She becomes gently persuasive.

SARAH   Sir, why don't we write to the publisher, and apologize for the delay, and tell him that you're back on track.

BIDDLE   I don't feel like it.

SARAH   I can tell that you don't, but sir, we are going to be absolutely defeated by this paperwork unless we— *(with fervor)* Lace the skates and hit the ice.

> *He looks at her, incredulously, his jaw almost dropping.*

BIDDLE   That's what all good Canadians would do.

SARAH   Yes, sir, all good Canadians worth their salt.

BIDDLE   Very well. *(starting for his desk)* What should I know about Saskatoon, Saskatchewan?

SARAH   *(getting her book)* Well, it's prairie. Wheat country. The provincial university is in Saskatoon. The city was incorporated in 1906.

BIDDLE   1906? Goodness me. I was twenty years old in 1906. Tell me this: What sort of people wanted to settle in Saskatoon, Saskatchewan?

SARAH   The first settlers were a "Temperance Colony." They were fleeing what they thought to be very liberal liquor laws in the east.

BIDDLE   And where did your people come from?

SARAH   Scotland, originally.

BIDDLE   Presbyterian?

SARAH   Yes. Well, I'd have to say lukewarm Presbyterian.

SARAH, with pad and pencil, sits down in front of his desk.

BIDDLE   Mine came from England. My first American ancestor, William Biddle, had been imprisoned as a dissenting Quaker. As had William Penn before him.

SARAH   *(ready to write)* May I have the name of your publisher?

BIDDLE   Alfred Knopf. This is very interesting. In 1681, William Biddle came across the pond and purchased, from William Penn, forty-three thousand acres of what is now New Jersey. Shortly after that the Biddles descended on Philadelphia.

SARAH   Do you have Knopf's address?

BIDDLE   *(He flashes the letter at her.)* Here is Knopf's address! Knopf's address is 201 East 55th. I think I should tell Alfred Knopf that I have a new secretary. "Mrs. Sarah-with-an-h-Schorr is late of Saskatchewan. Mrs. Schorr has an overbearing, Scots-Presbyterian manner."

There is a pause. SARAH is on the verge of tears.

If you're going to cry, *(pointing to the bathroom)* go in there.

SARAH   I'm not going to cry. If and when you make me cry I will sit right here in this chair, and cry.

BIDDLE   And make me bear witness.

SARAH   Yes, sir. *(quietly)* Sir, my father was a bully. I vowed, when I left Saskatoon, that I'd never allow another person to bully me. Please do not ask me for personal information and then make snide remarks.

BIDDLE   I didn't do that.

SARAH   Yes, you did. "Late of Saskatchewan." "Overbearing Scots-Presbyterian."

Silence, for a moment.

BIDDLE   You see, this tune-up this morning was a humdinger. Katherine is a well-balanced woman, normally, but on those occasions when she's surly, I tell you, the flies leave the room.

SARAH   Sir, we have a couple of possible solutions. If you will dictate as long as you can, I'll happily stay overtime, if necessary, and type the letters.

BIDDLE   You can stay until doomsday but the heat goes off at noon, when I leave.

SARAH   Very well. I don't mind taking the dictation home, and typing the letters there, and you will see that by Christmas we will keep that basket empty.

BIDDLE   I must say, you're inordinately anxious to work.

SARAH   Yes, sir. While I was growing up I was paid what is just about the best compliment you can get on the prairie. People said I was "a bugger for work."

BIDDLE laughs, for the first time.

BIDDLE   All right. Take this down, please. Speedily. "Dear Sam: I'm sorry to bore you with staff problems, indeed, I know it's unseemly to do so, but I've been having one devil of a time with secretaries. In June I had to fire a woman who was stupid in the extreme, and then, of course, we left for Cape Cod. When we returned, the September woman was an unmitigated disaster. Now, however, I've hired a young girl who is, in her own words, a bugger for work.

She will make sure that you receive the chapter about my ancestors before Christmas. Thank you for your patience. Sincerely, Francis." Type that up, please.

SARAH   Yes, sir.

          SARAH goes to her desk.

BIDDLE   Why did your father bully you?

SARAH   He was an alcoholic. He'd been fired from a rather prestigious position and it seems that, with the loss of the job, he lost his identity.

BIDDLE   Not unusual. Equating oneself with one's title is a particularly male affliction.

SARAH   Yes. He just locked himself in the house and drank. He actually bartered away the contents of our house for whisky.

BIDDLE   What do you mean, "contents"?

SARAH   Winchester rifles. Golf clubs. Silverware. I started working, part-time, when I was eleven.

BIDDLE   *(He pauses, examining her.)* Must have been very difficult.

SARAH   Yes, it was. My mother had to—

BIDDLE   *(sincerely)* Please, Sarah. On my knees, Sarah. Don't tell me more. I'm sorry, but I no longer have the resources.

          Brief pause.

          Surely you're not this candid with everyone?

SARAH   No, but I don't lie about it. It's who I am.

BIDDLE   You will find, as you go along, that you'll need one or two masks in your survival kit.

SARAH   Do you think so?

BIDDLE   I know so. It's the way the world functions. Now, I have to call Neilson, at the Pentagon. *(He reaches for his address book.)* He called two weeks ago but I've been too unravelled to return his call.

SARAH   Would you like me to place it?

BIDDLE   I would not. I've never approved of those gents who bellow, "Get me Wolfson at Interior, get me Robinson at State." I'm perfectly capable of making these calls myself. It is not, however, a pleasant procedure because my hands don't work. So I ask you, please, not to watch me.

> *SARAH looks through drawers. She assembles two pieces of paper with carbon paper in between.*

Did you hear me?

SARAH   Yes.

BIDDLE   Then, for God's sake, respond!

SARAH   I will not watch you!

BIDDLE   Thank you! Neilson at the Pentagon.

> *After finding the ten-digit number, he dials, wincing at the pain in his finger joints. SARAH keeps her head cocked at a peculiar angle, away from him.*

You're watching me!

SARAH   I am not!

BIDDLE   Hello? May I speak with—I'd like to speak with—

> *He is suddenly frightened.*

Just a moment.

> *He is lost and floundering. He turns and whispers to SARAH.*

Who?

SARAH   *(whispering, not looking)* Neilson.

BIDDLE   Kenneth Neilson, please. But it's ten o'clock in the morning—where could he be? Where? Boston. Yes, all right. Judge Biddle, Decatur 2-4858. But he mustn't call in the afternoon. I can only work from nine 'till noon. Yes. I'll be eighty-two next year. Thank you.

> *He hangs up, very depressed.*

That was one of my lapses. When I have them, I find myself floundering out there, in an ether. It's as if my mind excuses itself, without asking my permission. It just saunters off and thumbs its nose at me. Piss-a-dears. The strange thing is, a split second after the lapse, I can tell you that Kenneth Neilson's middle name is Maxwell, his wife's name is Marjorie, and they live at 1544 Halifax St.

> *He rises and shuffles around to the front of his desk. He turns SARAH's armless chair around, so that he faces her, and he sits.*

I'm going to come 'round and sit for a moment. This chair allows my arms to dangle and it relieves the pain in my hands.

> *He sits, with arms dangling, flexing his fingers.*
> *SARAH tries to type.*

Did you see the *Post* this morning?

SARAH   No, I didn't.

BIDDLE   Jacqueline Kennedy and Aristotle Onassis are an "item".

SARAH   *(hugely amazed)* I don't believe it!

BIDDLE   Katherine said, "Well, we always knew the Bouvier girls liked money, we just never knew how much."

> *SARAH smiles. He exhales deeply, wiggling his*
> *fingers.*

Didn't you tell me that you read poetry voluminously?

SARAH   Yes, I did.

BIDDLE   Who are your favourite poets?

SARAH   Edna St. Vincent Millay and e. e. cummings.

BIDDLE   Really? Odd juxtaposition. Cummings was at Harvard, you know. Class of 1915.

SARAH   Yes. I heard, on the radio this morning, that Lyndon Johnson's got ten thousand protesters in front of the White House today. Cummings had plenty to say on that subject.

BIDDLE   What subject?

SARAH   Civil disobedience.

BIDDLE   What, for instance?

SARAH   Well, one pungent line in particular comes to mind, but I'm afraid I can't repeat it.

BIDDLE   Repeat it, please.

SARAH   I can't, sir. It contains an obscenity.

BIDDLE   Oh, bosh and bunkum. Tell me.

SARAH   Are you sure?

BIDDLE   Positive.

SARAH   *(looking away)* "I will not kiss your fucking flag."

BIDDLE   *(smiling)* I'd forgotten that. It's from "I sing of Olaf glad and big", isn't it?

SARAH   Yes, sir.

BIDDLE   I think this, too, is from "Olaf". "There is some shit I will not eat."

SARAH   Yes, sir.

BIDDLE   Do you know, "Spring, when the world is mud-luscious and puddle wonderful."?

SARAH   Yes, I do.

A cloud of sadness comes across BIDDLE's face.

BIDDLE   Do you know, "King Christ, this world is all aleak, and life preservers there are none."?

SARAH   No, sir. Is it cummings?

BIDDLE   Yes. Katherine and I had two sons. We still have one. The other died at seven.

SARAH   I'm very sorry. What was his name?

BIDDLE   Garrison. Garrison Chapin Biddle. Forty years ago. Penicillin would have saved him but it wasn't available then. "Life preservers there were none." Did they give you any Shakespeare up there in Saskatoon?

SARAH   Yes, two plays a year for four years.

BIDDLE   I don't imagine you studied "King John"?

SARAH   No, sir.

BIDDLE   No. They only teach the crowd-pleasers. By the way, I forgot to tell you—that's the bathroom.

SARAH   Yes. Thank you.

BIDDLE   He says, in "King John":
"Grief fills the room up of my absent child,
Lies in his bed, walks up and down with me,
Puts on his pretty looks, repeats his words,
Remembers me of all his gracious parts,
Stuffs out his vacant garments with his form;
Then have I reason to be fond of grief."

> *SARAH waits, not knowing how to deal with his emotion. Eventually he makes "claws" of his hands.*

Who would have thought so much pain could be condensed in finger joints?

SARAH   Sir, my grandmother's hands were crippled with arthritis. The doctor told her to immerse them in oatmeal baths, but it didn't help. The only thing that really helped was massaging the knuckles with Ben Gay.

BIDDLE   I've got a tube of it in my desk drawer. But, to make a bad pun of it, here's the rub. How in hell can I massage the knuckles when it hurts to use my hands?

> *SARAH debates, for a moment, whether or not to give voice to her thought. She knows it is a precarious one.*

SARAH   *(quietly)* I could do it for you.

BIDDLE   *(whispering, incredulously)* I beg your pardon?

SARAH   *(cringing)* I just thought—

BIDDLE   Madam, you are bold as brass! I've never, ever, heard such a forward, ultimately embarrassing suggestion.

SARAH   I didn't mean to offend.

> *He rises and begins his shuffle back to his desk. He is indignant, SARAH is intimidated.*

BIDDLE   Well, you did! And it must never happen again. Do you hear me?

SARAH   Yes, sir. I'm sorry.

BIDDLE   *(He finds Monique's note.)* And what the hell does Cook want?

SARAH   A cheque.

BIDDLE   A cheque? What for? I paid them on the first of the month.

> *A fearful pause.*

Didn't I?

SARAH   Yes, you did.

A moment passes as he reads Monique's request.

BIDDLE God-a-mighty, she must think that *I* am Aristotle Onassis! I have never, in fifty-five years of hiring servants, had to pay for their shoe leather. She says that the shoes they wear are worn performing household services and therefore it is only just—just, mind you, that I give her a hundred dollars to keep them shod.

SARAH Sir, try not to let this—

BIDDLE Don't nag at me! Did you do that to your grandmother? Did you nag her to death? I'm going to call Bill Bullitt.

He looks for his address book.

Bullitt was Ambassador to France, after Moscow. He hired them in Paris, and brought them over when he came back.

He finds his book.

I tell you, if William Bullitt says he bought their shoes, I will rise like a phoenix and go right through this ceiling. Bullitt, Bullitt—

He has found the "B's". There is a pause.

There's a line through it.

SARAH reaches for a phone book.

SARAH Is he unlisted, or would he be in the book?

BIDDLE He's in the cemetery. He died last February. Katherine and I went to the service.

Holding up the book.

Do you see this? Do you see all these lines? All the B's are dead.

He turns the page.

Can you believe it?

Incredulously.

Surely they can't be.

He squints and runs his finger down both pages.

But they are. All the B's are dead.

SARAH   I'm sorry.

> *As he registers the enormity of what he's said, he becomes deeply depressed. He rises and begins his shuffle to the closest heater.*

Sir, what are you doing?

BIDDLE   I'm shutting off the heat and calling it a day.

SARAH   Oh, please, sir, don't. Let's discuss Cook's request.

BIDDLE   The woman is a succubus! I already provide them with wine at lunch and dinner. They say it's their Gallic birthright. They say that, without it, they'll develop ulcers. Get your coat. We're finished here.

> *He leans on the chair and bends down to the dial.*

SARAH   Sir, we really do need to answer Professor Pearlman's inquiry about Justice Frankfurter.

BIDDLE   What is that? The royal "we"? You may need to, but I have no such need. These historians push and poke and prod and then get it all wrong, anyway. Oh, what the hell, I suppose, for accuracy, I should answer. Get your book.

SARAH   He wanted to know if—

BIDDLE   I remember what he wanted to know. Take this down, and I leave it to you to plug in the niceties.

> *As he rises from the first heater, he rattles off the following very fast.*

"Yes, in 1940 Felix Frankfurter recommended, to President Roosevelt, that I be appointed Solicitor General. A year later I was, of course, appointed Attorney General."

SARAH   Sir, you're going too fast.

> *As he heads for the second heater.*

BIDDLE   It wouldn't be, if you'd learned Gregg.

> *Dictating again.*

"We had known each other long before our Washington days because of our mutual connection to Harvard Law. I had graduated in 1911 and Felix became a professor there as early as 1914. I hope you find this information adequate. Sincerely, etc."

> *Brief pause.*

We have now answered the inquiry. Go and get your coat.

> *SARAH, unwillingly, leaves her desk and goes to the hanger.*

And when you go through the kitchen, I want you to muster every bit of Canadian civility that you possess, and tell the succubus to take up the shoe matter with Mrs. Biddle.

SARAH   *(dressing)* Sir, she said she did that, back in October, and Mrs. Biddle assured her that you'd give her a cheque.

BIDDLE   What? Are you telling me that Katherine agreed to keeping them shod?

SARAH   Yes, sir.

> *BIDDLE has shut off the second heater.*

BIDDLE   God-a-mighty! You know what that means. It means another damned tune-up at dinner time. It is absolutely crushing. *(He heads for the hanger.)* If you're ready to go, go!

SARAH   May I type the letters at home?

BIDDLE   *(putting on his earmuffs)* Are you going to charge me overtime?

SARAH   No, sir.

BIDDLE   Very well, take your book.

> *SARAH gets her steno pad and puts it into her shoulder bag.*

And take the thermos tray.

SARAH   Yes, sir.

> *She sees him struggling with his coat. His right arm is in the sleeve but his left arm can't locate the left sleeve. SARAH goes to assist.*

Sir, may I help—

BIDDLE   Do not touch me! I may be an invalid but I'm not yet entirely in-valid.

> *There is a silence as SARAH gets the tray and the mail sack. She then approaches the door.*

SARAH   Goodbye.

BIDDLE   Goodbye.

> *She exits. We hear her going down the stairs. As she nears the bottom of the stairs, BIDDLE shuffles over and opens the door.*

Sarah?

SARAH   *(offstage)* Yes, sir?

BIDDLE   I am *not* your grandmother.

SARAH   *(offstage)* No, sir.

> *Blackout.*

ACT ONE

SCENE THREE

> *It is two weeks later, 9:00 A.M., BIDDLE is seated
> at his desk, reading the* Washington Post. *He has
> a handkerchief and wipes his nose frequently.
> SARAH runs up the stairs and enters. While jug-
> gling a 9 x 12 envelope, she places the thermos tray.
> She leaves the mail sack, as well as the envelope, at
> BIDDLE's desk. She then removes her coat at the
> hanger. BIDDLE has, more than we've seen before,
> a very short fuse.*

SARAH   Good morning.

BIDDLE   Good morning.

SARAH   How are you today?

BIDDLE   Not good. I've got the sinus drip. The doctor says it
will pass. As will life, I told him. Gene McCarthy's
announced his candidacy. Won't be nominated.

> *She gives him the envelope of letters.*

SARAH   Bobby Kennedy will?

BIDDLE   Maybe. Maybe Hubert Humphrey. How was your
Thanksgiving?

> *She had hoped he wouldn't ask. She answers
> tremulously.*

SARAH   Oh…. It was all right. We had to go up to Yale again.

> *She is surprised to find herself on the verge of tears.*

My husband had a meeting about his dissertation.

BIDDLE   You're upset.

SARAH   I'm sorry.

BIDDLE   *(irritably)* Because you were deprived of a turkey dinner?

SARAH   *(snapping back)* No, sir, because the trip was... *(with quivering lip)* difficult. Just the two of us, in the car, for all those hours.

BIDDLE   Please don't burden me with it.

SARAH   No, sir.

BIDDLE   I have very little strength and what I have is precious.

> *He hauls a six-hundred page manuscript in front of him.*

And I'm still wading through this tome about the Japanese internment. *(opening the envelope)* Is this the work you did at home?

SARAH   Yes, sir. Three letters that need your signature.

BIDDLE   *(frowning)* Three?

SARAH   Yes, sir. One was to Mr. Neilson at the Pentagon, one to Dillon Ripley at the Smithsonian, and one to Ruth Stern.

BIDDLE   Why did I write Ruth Stern?

SARAH   She inquired about the time you spent as secretary to Oliver Wendell Holmes.

BIDDLE   Justice Holmes, to you, Madam.

SARAH   Yes, sir. Justice Holmes.

He proceeds to sign the letters.

BIDDLE   I don't understand why you have to do so much work at home.

SARAH   *(gently)* I… can't seem to… manage to… get it done here.

BIDDLE   Well, let's hope that your recognition of the problem leads to improvement.

SARAH   Yes, sir.

> *Brief pause.*

Sir, we're making good headway on the memoirs. May we continue?

BIDDLE   Are you deaf? I just said that I'm critiquing this manuscript about the Japanese internment.

SARAH   Sir, wouldn't it be more productive if we reserved the time that I'm here for dictation?

BIDDLE   I intuit that you're in your "persistent mode."God knows, Hell hath no fury like Sarah in her persistent mode. Bring your book.

SARAH   Thank you. How was your Thanksgiving?

BIDDLE   Not good. One of my nephews brought bad news about a great-nephew. I'm going to have to write my lawyer and change my will.

> *SARAH is now seated.*

Ready?

SARAH   Yes, sir.

BIDDLE   My father died when I was six years old, leaving my thirty-two-year-old mother with four boys.

         BIDDLE holds his stomach.

SARAH   Sir, what is it?

BIDDLE   Blocked... intestines.

SARAH   Sir, chamomile—

BIDDLE   *(holding up a hand)* Please don't tell me your Granny's remedy.

SARAH   Is there anything I can do?

BIDDLE   You can take this down. "In 1899, when I was thirteen, I was sent to board at Groton, north of Boston. I remained there for six years, until 1905. In 1905 we still used horses and buggies, and Mark Twain was still alive. Leo Tolstoy was still alive." New paragraph. "Franklin Roosevelt had been at Groton before me. I was a new boy when Franklin was a sixth former. He told me, in later years, that he enjoyed it. I did not enjoy it. I found the place to be bleak and austere, entirely without embellishment. There was not one whit of privacy—I was surrounded by a melee of boys every hour of the day—and yet I was always lonely.

         There is another stomach "twinge." He waits until
         it passes.

I recall being herded, at the crack of dawn, toward rows of metal sinks that held chunks of harsh, yellow soap. After morning wash we'd put on our little blue suits with the Eton collars, and listen to the Reverend Endicott Peabody tell us that what American boys lacked was tone."

Pause.

I think I can't continue. Go and type it up.

SARAH rises from her chair.

SARAH Endicott has two 't's'?

BIDDLE Yes. The Reverend Endicott Peabody damn near killed me with his sanctimonious religiosity. He knew and taught and understood one thing only. He called it "muscular Christianity." *(muttering to himself)* Please, God, on my knees, God, let me depart this earth without ever again experiencing "muscular Christianity."

> *He looks at SARAH. She has not returned to her desk, as expected. She hesitates, wanting to resolve the "shoe matter."*

(impatiently) Well? Go type it up.

SARAH Before I do, sir, Cook stopped me again as I went through the kitchen. She insists on a cheque for the shoes.

BIDDLE I'm at the end of my tether with that clucking Frenchwoman! *(irritably)* What do you think I should do?

SARAH Do you really want my opinion?

BIDDLE Yes, yes, yes!

SARAH I think one has to consider the psychic toll.

BIDDLE The psychic toll.

SARAH Yes.

BIDDLE   Bosh and bunkum.

SARAH   Sir, if you let this sit there and fester, it will affect your other activities. But if you write the cheque you can erase it from your slate. And really, it's a very minor matter.

BIDDLE   It isn't minor. It's a matter of principle. I'm not like Groucho Marx, *(mimicing Marx)* "If you don't like my principles, I have others." Please be seated.

   SARAH sits, once again.

SARAH   Yes, sir.

BIDDLE   This is to Robert Henderson, Esquire. "Dear Bob: Sorry to say I need another codicil to my will. John was here at Thanksgiving and he did not bring tidings of great joy about Michael. Michael has gone too far this time. He's using drugs. I want him out immediately, and I want his ten thousand to go to the Memorial Library. This latter, however, I want *inter vivos*. Please send a letter of confirmation. Thank you. Sincerely. Francis." Type that first, and then the memoirs. No, wait a minute. Take this down before I forget it. I remembered it this morning. It's for later in the memoirs.

   Pause.

   "Hermann Wilhelm Goering wore the double-breasted light gray uniform of a Reich Marshal. It was faded and baggy and without decorations. He sat in the corner of the defendant's box with a rug across his knees." Save that, please, in the Nuremberg folder.

SARAH   Yes, sir.

BIDDLE immediately pulls the "Japanese internment" manuscript in front of him and begins to read.

SARAH goes directly to a large dictionary that is placed on a stand. BIDDLE looks up from the manuscript and notices her at the dictionary.

BIDDLE   What are you doing? What can't you spell?

SARAH   *Inter vivos.* I don't know if it's two words and I don't know what it means.

BIDDLE   *(holding his stomach)* Of course you don't. Your knowledge is, to put it kindly, somewhat circum-scribed. Due to the influence of Saskatchewan, no doubt.

SARAH   *(in anger and disbelief)* Judge Biddle, I will not listen to—

BIDDLE   Oh, don't be so belligerently sensitive! I think we can safely say, without insult, that I have forgotten more in the last year than you've learned in all of your twenty-five. If you weren't so damned obtuse you'd decipher it. *Inter vivos.* In life. While living. I want the money to pass to the Memorial Library now, before I die.

The phone rings. SARAH goes to her desk.

Hello? Of course he's here, you're speaking with him.

He listens.

Yes, I sent four cheques, dividend cheques. Yes. To be deposited in my personal account.

He frowns.

They aren't? I must have forgotten them. You see, I'll be eighty-two next year. Let me tell you what happens. It's as if my mind excuses itself without asking my permission. Saunters off and thumbs its nose at me. Yes, I will. Thank you.

He hangs up.

I sent a deposit slip to the bank, listing four cheques. I didn't send the cheques. I didn't send them and I have no idea where they are. Check your book to see if I listed them.

SARAH   Sir, I have only the household chequebook. You would have logged them into your personal chequebook, at the house.

BIDDLE   *(angrily)* And do you know why my personal chequebook has to be kept at the house?

SARAH   No, sir.

BIDDLE   Because I couldn't trust that imbecile secretary! She blabbed my personal finances all over town. Actually told the clucking succubus how much IBM I owned. And when I refused to raise her wage she said, "Sir, if you can contribute five hundred dollars to the Mozart Society, surely you can give me a raise."

He rises, becoming irrational.

The city teems with them, you know. Retired, desiccated, civil servants. They spend thirty years in government cubicles and then they get themselves tight little permanent waves and come to me. And set the place on fire.

He starts for a heater.

It's too hot in here.

SARAH   *(dreading the "heater routine")* Sir, really, it's quite
             comfortable.

BIDDLE   Oh, don't be so damned contrary. I'll just turn this
             one down.

             Seeing her forlorn face.

             Look for the cheques, girl! Look for the cheques.

             *SARAH, at her desk, lifts the "house" phone, and
             buzzes. BIDDLE performs his heater routine.*

SARAH   *(on the phone)* Mrs. Biddle, it's Sarah.

BIDDLE   *(bending at the heater)* What in hell are you doing?

SARAH   *(on the phone)* I'm sorry to bother you but we've just
             had a call from the bank, regarding the personal
             account. Yes, dividend cheques. The deposit slip was
             sent but the cheques weren't. There were four. Could
             I ask you, please, to try and locate them? Thank you.

             She hangs up.

BIDDLE   How dare you include Katherine in this fiasco!

SARAH   Sir, the cheques have to be found.

BIDDLE   Well then, find them!

SARAH   I can't find them! I'm not permitted to find them!
             They're in your office at the house.

BIDDLE   What insolence! *(wailing, childishly)* All I wanted was
             an obedient, pliable clerk for a period of one year!
             You are not pliable. You are the most trying
             individual I have ever had the misfortune to know.
             Really, I don't know what was in Katherine's head.
             I need a God-damned cup of coffee.

He shuffles to the table.

SARAH   *(rising)* May I get that for—

BIDDLE   You may not! And since you came in here today chomping at the bit for a tune-up, I'll give you one! I can not, I will not, leave that blanket dismissal of yours unaddressed any longer.

SARAH   What blanket dismissal?

BIDDLE   The "pleated-plaid Ivy girl" dismissal. *(mimicing)* "No, sir, I'm not one of those." It's nothing but sour grapes. Chip-on-the-shoulder, nose-out-of-joint, blatant sour grapes.

She takes him on.

SARAH   Judge Biddle, I'm a prairie populist. It was hard for me, at the ad agency, to see the Smithies being promoted just because they were Smithies. I believe that one has to zealously take issue with unfair practices—

BIDDLE   "To zealously take issue" is a split infinitive! Split infinitives were not allowed at Groton.

SARAH   Sir, I believe that one has to take issue zealously with unfair practices. And I think it's important to take issue zealously with this cherished eastern belief that one's worth is measured by one's school. Or worse, that one's worth is measured by one's ancestors. The measure of one's worth is the measure of one's journey.

BIDDLE   One's journey.

SARAH   Yes. The distance between one's origins and one's accomplishments. For instance, if a Black man, whose great-grandparents were slaves, graduates from college, that accomplishment is more impressive than when a White man, when a White man—

She is unable to stop her thought.

Whose family began with forty-three thousand acres of what is now New Jersey, graduates from Harvard.

There is a pause. Both are stunned that she has gone this far.

BIDDLE   Young woman, and I don't mean young lady, you need to be reminded that I was fifty-six years old when you were still on the potty. And you need to understand that there is no conversation that you and I might have, regardless of the topic, no conversation that I have not had, verbatim in all likelihood, with some other person in some other decade. So the probability is that all conversation between us will be, for me, tiresome.

SARAH   *(holding her ground)* "Young woman, and I don't mean young lady," is not only outmoded, it is elitist, eastern-establishment snobbery.

BIDDLE   You see? I've had this identical conversation with Harry Truman and Hubert Humphrey.

SARAH   I'm not surprised. Neither man was Ivy League.

BIDDLE   Madam, your tenacity defeats me! How can this be? How can it be that I, who have sat in a German court-room facing the likes of Goering and Hess and Speer and Ribbentrop, can allow myself to be defeated by a callow girl on a soap box with a sermon?

SARAH   Sir, when I say that I am "not one of those," and you call that statement "sour grapes," you imply that, if I don't covet an Ivy League education, I should. And that is contrary to all of your words and all of your deeds over fifty years of this century. Have you forgotten your commitment to the Pennsylvania coal miners?

BIDDLE   Have you forgotten your much-vaunted Canadian civility? It has shrivelled up and piss-ad-eared into thin air!

SARAH   Oh, for God's sake, sir, I went to the library! I got Walker's biography. You were "Main Line" Philadelphia! When you joined the Democratic party the Republicans called you a "radical patrician." They said you were a traitor to your class. When you chaired the National Labor Relations Board the Democrats called you, "the noblest Roman of them all." Are you no longer a Democrat? *(She is near tears.)* Have you become nothing more than a hectoring, domineering old man?

BIDDLE   I can't believe my ears. I should terminate you here and now and save us both a heap of grief. You are an insufferable shrew! Is it any wonder that your father bullied you?

> *A moment passes as SARAH gazes at him in disbelief.*

SARAH   I beg your pardon?

BIDDLE   I swear, you'll be driving me to drink by Christmas!

> *Slowly, methodically, she finds her handbag, and then marches to the bentwood hanger.*

What does this mean? Are you quitting?

SARAH   Sir, I know.

BIDDLE   Know what?

SARAH   I know that the last two unmitigated disasters were not "terminated." They resigned. I knew that when I accepted the job.

BIDDLE   Katherine.

SARAH   Yes, sir.

BIDDLE   Betraying me.

SARAH   No, sir. Trying to paint an accurate picture of what the
          job entailed. And I said, "Well, Mrs. Biddle, we
          Saskatchewan girls are known for our grit, so I will
          try." But, sir, *(as she puts on her coat)* "There is some
          shit I will not eat."

                    There is a long, agonized pause.

BIDDLE   You can't quit. You just can't. If you do, I'll die all the
          sooner. If you promise not to, I will promise to try
          harder.

SARAH   But, sir, I seem to rankle you at every turn.

BIDDLE   Sarah, I'm asking you, please, to gird yourself with all
          of your youthful stamina and stay with me for the
          duration.

                    *He waits, expectantly, for a reply. SARAH is in
                    a quandary.*

          Do you want to go home, and think about it
          overnight?

SARAH   Sir, will you really, really try?

BIDDLE   I will. I'll try, try and try again.

SARAH   Very well.

                    *She removes her coat and says the following,
                    emphatically.*

I'll go and type the *inter vivos* letter. And, sir, once that machine starts clacking, I'll ask you please to let me type the damn letter without interruption.

BIDDLE Of course. Thank you.

> *SARAH goes to her desk. She begins to type, reading from her steno book.*

Excuse me?

SARAH Yes, sir?

BIDDLE If you'll bring me the book I'll write a cheque for Cook.

> *SARAH sits, rigidly.*

I'm sorry I've interrupted you. I thought you'd be pleased. Please bring me the book.

SARAH I would prefer not to.

BIDDLE I beg your pardon?

SARAH I have finally reconciled the chequebook. If you want me to be responsible for the household finances, you must let me write the cheques.

BIDDLE But it's my house and my servant and—

> *A pause. He swallows hard.*

And of course you're right. You will write the cheque.

SARAH Yes, sir, thank you. I'll do that when I've finished this letter.

> *SARAH continues typing.*

BIDDLE   But of course, you don't have power of attorney.

SARAH   No, sir.

BIDDLE   So you can write the cheque but you can't actually sign it.

SARAH   No, sir.

BIDDLE   No, only I can do that.

SARAH   Yes, sir.

> *She continues typing. BIDDLE pretends to read the "Japanese" manuscript but can't keep up the pretense.*

BIDDLE   Sarah?

SARAH   Yes, sir?

BIDDLE   Truly, I don't always have to have the last word, but not only did cummings go to Harvard, St. Vincent Millay went to Vassar.

SARAH   Sir, the schools they attended aren't really relevant. Literature can be taught, Physics can be taught, talent can't be taught.

> *BIDDLE thinks about this, briefly.*

BIDDLE   *Touché*, my dear, *touché*.

> *Again, SARAH types. BIDDLE is deeply moved by her trip to the library.*

Sarah?

SARAH   Yes, sir?

BIDDLE   You read Walker's biography of me?

SARAH   Yes, sir.

BIDDLE   All of it?

SARAH   Yes, sir.

BIDDLE   Cover to cover?

SARAH   Yes, sir.

BIDDLE   *(His eyes well up with tears.)* Thank you.

SARAH   You're welcome.

BIDDLE   *(wiping his eyes)* Goddamn sinus drip.

CURTAIN

ACT TWO

SCENE ONE

It is the beginning of January, 1968. The bentwood hanger holds the usual paraphernalia. BIDDLE's desk is no longer the mess it was in Act One.

As the curtain rises we see SARAH and BIDDLE standing at a table that holds a portable dictaphone. Please note that "Ginn's" Office Supply is a hard "g", as in gun.

BIDDLE I absolutely, categorically, will not use the damn thing! I'd as soon throw it in the rubbish.

SARAH Sir, you can't. It was a Christmas present. And a very expensive one at that.

BIDDLE I don't know what was in Katherine's head!

SARAH Couldn't we just try?

BIDDLE There you go again with your royal "we." No, we can not. You must remember, Sarah, that at one time I learned to talk into a telephone. That was, shall we say, admissable, because there was a human being at the other end. I can not and will not make conversation with a machine.

SARAH But they're so easy to use. All you do is push this button to start the tape, and then you talk into this microphone.

BIDDLE What the hell's the advantage of it?

SARAH Well, you're here a half hour before I am. You could dictate while you're waiting. Or when I go to the Post Office. And then, when I return, I'd play it back and transcribe it. I'd wear these earphones, so you wouldn't hear anything, and you could concentrate on reading correspondence and manuscripts.

BIDDLE   Show me how it works.

> *SARAH takes the microphone, pushes the button and speaks.*

SARAH   Happy New Year, Mr. Dictaphone. It is January, 1968. You have been rescued from the shelves at Ginn's, and now you are free to happily and gainfully reside here, in Judge Biddle's office.

> *She shuts it off.*

BIDDLE   Perhaps you don't actually know what a split infinitive is. When you insert an adverb between to, and the verb, reside, you are splitting the infinitive. So it isn't, "You are free to happily and gainfully reside," it's, "You are free to reside happily and gainfully."

SARAH   Yes, I'm sorry. I forget sometimes.

BIDDLE   It's a thorn in my side.

SARAH   Yes, I'm sorry. Now if we want to listen to what I said— *(pushing a button)* We push this to rewind—

> *Brief pause.*

And when you hear that click, you can play it back.

> *She starts it again. We hear SARAH's voice, coming from the dictaphone.*

"Happy New Year, Mr. Dictaphone. It is January, 1968. You have been rescued from the shelves at Ginn's, and now you are free to happily and gainfully reside here, in Judge Biddle's office."

She shuts it off.

You see? Easy as pie. They're being used very widely now.

BIDDLE   Amazing. It's an amazing gadget altogether. How would you remove what you just said?

SARAH   You'd rewind and then speak over it. Once you got the hang of it, you might even want to take it to the house and dictate there.

BIDDLE   Never. Never in a million years. What if someone came into the room and found me talking to it? They'd think I was certifiable.

SARAH   Please, sir—

BIDDLE   Sarah, do not harp on this string! I'm too old a dog to learn new tricks. Get your book.

He limps to his desk.

I'm feeling surprisingly lucid this morning, and I think I can do a good letter.

As SARAH sits.

This is to Professor Shiko Furukawa, Stanford University. "I am returning herewith your manuscript, 'Insult and Injury'. It's a very fine piece of work and there is little to carp about. You mention Colonel Bendetsen. May I call your attention to his entry in the 1948-49 edition of *Who's Who?* It states that Bendetsen—

(to SARAH) Did you find it?

SARAH flips a couple of pages in her book.

SARAH   Yes.

BIDDLE   Read it, please.

SARAH   *(reading)* "Colonel Bendetson conceived the method,
formulated the details, and directed the evacuation of
125,000 persons of Japanese ancestry."

BIDDLE   Good. Slip it in there.

(continuing dictation) "In the next edition of *Who's
Who*, Bendetson had all references to the internment
removed. Shortly thereafter, the American Civil
Liberties Union called the internment 'the worst
single wholesale violation of civil rights of American
citizens in our history.'"

Pause.

New paragraph. "As I expressed to you on the phone,
any man who goes to his grave without regrets is
a man who has failed to comprehend his life. My
conscience reviews the internment almost daily, and
daily I conclude that I failed miserably. My own
deepest regret is that my vehement objections fell on
deaf ears, and Henry Stimson, the Secretary of War,
prevailed. Never again will I trust that mystic cliché,
'military necessity'."

Pause.

New paragraph. "I should forewarn you, since this is
your first foray into publishing, that some of the
critics will find 'Insult and Injury' inordinately
impassioned. You must, of course, ignore them. It is
a given that this book could not have been born without your particular brain—

Pause. He thinks.

Without your particular brain—

Pause.

Without your particular brain, and your particular blood. Sincerely, etcetera." Type that up please.

SARAH   Yes, sir.

> *She goes to her desk, lays down her book, and realizes that a dam of tears is about to burst.*

Would you excuse me for a moment?

BIDDLE   Certainly.

> *SARAH exits into the bathroom. BIDDLE opens an envelope, takes out a letter, and then gazes rather wickedly at the dictaphone.*
>
> *He rises, holding the letter, and limps over to the dictaphone. He glances at the bathroom door. He rewinds the tape, then lifts the microphone and pushes the start button.*

Mr. Dictaphone, this is Judge Biddle. I've come to right a wrong.

> *Pause.*

That's why God created Democrats.

> *He laughs.*

Mr. Dictaphone, you've been rescued from the shelves at Ginn's and now you are free to reside, happily and gainfully, here in my office.

> *He pushes the stop button and starts back to his desk. He pauses near the bathroom. He had expected SARAH to come out by now.*

Sarah-with-an-h? Are you all right?

SARAH   *(offstage)* Yes, sir. I'll be out in a minute.

BIDDLE   I'm sorry I was so intractable about the dictaphone. I promise to try it later this morning.

SARAH   Thank you.

> *He switches the letter to his left hand in order to flex the fingers on his right hand. He then heads for SARAH's chair.*

BIDDLE   Best to dangle the hands a bit.

> *He sits in SARAH's chair, returning to the letter.*

Dear, dear, dear. Symphony, ballet, opera, theatre. Always in need of money.

> *Shaking his head.*

Never understood it, myself. Wrong-headed government priorities. Thought I might, eventually, if I lived long enough. Never will now. Who said it? Dos Passos? "All we can learn about all who have gone before us, we learn from the art they've left us."

> *He thinks.*

Something similar, something trenchant, somewhere in Dobson. Can't remember.

> *Looking toward a bookshelf.*

Where the hell's the *Bartlett's*?

He rises and limps toward a bookshelf. He stops, looks at the bathroom door, shakes his head and frowns.

Something's amok. Probably just the monthly, female thing.

(He continues to the bookshelf.) Henry Austin Dobson. Used to know it by heart.

(He finds Bartlett's.) Here it is. Scorched.

(He smells the book.) I can still smell the smoke.

(He looks up Dobson.) Droit, gauche.

(He shakes his head.) Simple enough but she couldn't get it through her thick skull.

(He finds the passage.) Here we are.

(He reads.) "All passes. Art alone enduring stays to us; the bust outlasts the throne, the coin, Tiberius."

(He smiles, nodding his agreement.) Yes.

(He replaces the book.) And Franklin remains on the dime.

SARAH comes out of the bathroom and goes directly to her desk. She has been crying. During the following, she sets up her papers and carbon.

BIDDLE starts back to his desk.

Did you ever read *The Maxims of Marcel Proust*?

SARAH   No, sir.

BIDDLE   Proust says a wonderful thing about the endurance of
art. Haven't looked at Proust in fifty years, so why
I remember it is a mystery. "Through all of the
centuries, Rembrandt and Vermeer continue to send
us their special rays."

SARAH   That's lovely.

SARAH doubles over in a flood of anguished tears.

I'm sorry! I'm so sorry.

BIDDLE   Goodness. Goodness me.

She continues to cry.

Dear, dear, dear.

SARAH   Forgive me. I'm sorry.

BIDDLE   Please, no need to apologize. Was I hectoring again,
about the split infinitives?

SARAH   No, sir, it's not that.

*There is an awkward moment of silence, but for the
tears.*

BIDDLE   *(quietly)* Is it—is it the monthly, female thing?

*Inexplicably, she begins to laugh. She laughs and
cries and laughs and cries. She reaches into her bag
for Kleenex.*

SARAH   Yes, it is! It's the absence of it. I'm pregnant.

BIDDLE   Ah. Well, I, I don't know what to say. I mean, there's
so much one could say, but all of the things one
usually says, well, I think they're not appropriate.

Pause.

When are you expecting?

SARAH   July.

> *SARAH blows her nose and wipes her eyes.*
> *BIDDLE inhales and exhales, becoming flustered.*

BIDDLE   The fact is, I simply cannot engage the idea of a new life.

SARAH   Yes, sir. I understand.

BIDDLE   If I do, if I even contemplate all the ramifications of a birth, I'll be drawn into the morass.

SARAH   I know, sir.

BIDDLE   I can not allow myself to be embroiled in—even to be on the periphery of your domestic difficulties.

SARAH   Nor should you, sir. I'm sorry I—

BIDDLE   I have very little strength, and what I have is precious.

SARAH   Yes, sir.

BIDDLE   So I must ask you, please, Sarah, on my knees, Sarah, do not drag me into your problems.

SARAH   No, sir. I won't. I'm all right now. Really, I am.

> *SARAH inserts the paper and begins typing.*
> *BIDDLE rises and heads for the coffee table.*
> *SARAH stops typing.*

(rising) May I get—

BIDDLE   (*pouring his own coffee*) I want you to understand that it's not that I'm indifferent. It's that I'm in the process of leaving this life. The exit sign is flashing over the door and the door is ajar.

SARAH   Sir, I do understand. I'm very sorry for the outburst.

BIDDLE   What I mean is, discussion of these huge, life issues exacts a toll. (*grudgingly*) A psychic toll.

SARAH   Yes, sir.

BIDDLE   (*moving to his desk*) Please, go ahead and type the letter.

> *SARAH types a few sentences while he makes his way back to his desk. He sits for only a moment and then:*

Sarah? Come over here.

> *She rises, with her book.*

You needn't bring your book.

> *She sits in front of him.*

SARAH   Yes, sir?

BIDDLE   Sarah, it's the universal pattern. As if we're all on the same road on some obligatory map. We're born, we marry, we make our replacements, and then we die.

SARAH   Yes, sir.

BIDDLE   We have no say in the way we're born and we have no say in the way we die.

SARAH   Yes, sir.

BIDDLE   And as we age all we can do is wonder how it will
                  happen. In a bed in your home, or a bed at the
                  hospital. Or at the dinner table. Or jay-walking on
                  Main Street.

                  Pause.

                  I'm sorry. Lately, no matter where I start, I wind up
                  wondering how it's going to end.

                  Pause.

                  Sometime in the future you want to write seriously.

SARAH   Yes, sir, I do.

BIDDLE   You envision that as a part of your "journey"?

SARAH   Yes, sir.

BIDDLE   Well, you mustn't think you can't pursue it because of
                  the baby. You'll hire a nanny.

SARAH   I don't know, sir. Where I come from we raise our
                  own children.

BIDDLE   Well, then, you'll just have to hold it in abeyance for
                  awhile. Abeyance is a woman's plight. Biology
                  decided that, Betty Friedan notwithstanding.

                  Pause.

                  Is it possible for you to tell me what the problem is,
                  briefly, in one sentence?

                  SARAH thinks a moment.

SARAH   I am very lonely in my marriage.

BIDDLE   You're both very young, and he's just starting out. That might change.

SARAH   I don't think it's likely.

There is a brief pause.

BIDDLE   Katherine and I lost a son in 1930. He was seven years old.

SARAH   Yes, sir.

BIDDLE   Penicillin could have saved him.

SARAH   Yes, sir. "Life preservers there were none."

BIDDLE suddenly rests his head in his hands.

BIDDLE   I—I just don't have the resources for this. I just don't.

SARAH   Sir, really, I do understand.

BIDDLE   No, I don't think you can. You're at a disadvantage, in that I have been young, but you have never been old. I have to call a friend at Justice. You'd best go finish the Furukawa letter.

SARAH   *(rising)* Yes, sir. Sir, do you mean Melvin Grainger, at Justice?

BIDDLE   Yes, I need to call him.

SARAH   Sir, are you sure?

BIDDLE   Of course I'm sure. He resigned, just before Christmas. I want to praise the job he's done and say goodbye.

SARAH   Sir, you already did. Just before Christmas.

BIDDLE   I couldn't have! I composed what I wanted to say over Christmas.

He gets his address book.

Grainger. Justice.

SARAH   Sir, you called and you quoted President Wilson. You said that, "when a man comes to Washington, he either swells or he grows."

BIDDLE closes his address book.

BIDDLE   You're saying I have had that conversation.

SARAH   Yes, sir.

BIDDLE   You're positive.

SARAH   Yes, sir.

BIDDLE   The swells or grows conversation.

SARAH   Yes, sir. You complimented Mr. Grainger by saying that he'd grown, not swelled.

BIDDLE shakes his head, in forlorn exasperation.

BIDDLE   All right, then, tell me. Have I already written the man on Seventy-Eighth Street?

SARAH   I'm sorry, sir, I don't know which man you—

BIDDLE   The "Eleanor" man, in New York City! He's got to be taken to task.

SARAH   No, sir, you haven't. *(going to BIDDLE's desk)* Let me find his letter so that—

BIDDLE   I remember his letter!

SARAH   Sir, you're upset. I know what you're going to say, so
           why don't you let me write that letter? And then you
           can sort through the mail.

BIDDLE   And now, in addition to being a bugger for work,
           you're clairvoyant. You do not know what I'm going
           to say.

SARAH   Oh, yes, I do. I know that what you're going to say is
           not about Mrs. Roosevelt.

BIDDLE   Sarah, when you're in your persistent mode, the flies
           leave the room. *(rising)* I'm going to try the dicta-
           phone, but I can't have you typing at the same time.

SARAH   *(pleased that he'll try)* No, sir. I have bills to pay. I can
           type later.

BIDDLE   *(rising from his desk)* Nothing ventured, nothing
           gained.

SARAH   Yes, sir. Thank you very much for trying.

BIDDLE   Faint heart ne'er won fair maiden.

SARAH   Yes, sir.

BIDDLE   *(at the dictaphone)* So all I do is push the button and
           start?

SARAH   That's all.

           *He takes hold of the microphone. Smiling, he turns
           to SARAH.*

BIDDLE   Does this make me a "dictatOR"? You'd best not
           answer that.

           (pushing the "Start" button) "Dear Whats-his-name: In
           your letter of whenever-it-was, you say, 'I brought the

Eleanor Roosevelt manuscript to the Editor-in-Chief and he was pleased.' I'm sorry, but I'm compelled to correct you. You didn't bring the manuscript, you took the manuscript. Bring is used only when something is brought to you. The Editor-in-Chief might say, 'Bring me the manuscript'. You would take it to him. Whereupon you would say, 'I took the manuscript to the Editor-in-Chief,' and he would say, 'He brought the manuscript to me'."

Pause.

New paragraph. "This mis-use of bring-and-take is common in New York City, and it's a thorn in my side. And, since everything that happens in New York City eventually emanates to the rest of country—mostly, of course, from Madison Avenue—it is particularly dangerous to perpetuate this bastardization of our language. Sincerely."

He stops the machine.

I leave it to you to plug in the niceties.

SARAH   Yes, sir, I will.

BIDDLE   *(in a sing-song)* "Good luck, take heart, press on, all best," etcetera, etcetera.

          He grimaces and grasps his knees, in pain.

I have to stretch out.

SARAH   All right, sir.

          He hobbles over to the cot and lies down. He has to bend his knees to do so and he grimaces.

BIDDLE   Got a list of ailments from here to Mt. Rushmore.

Brief pause.

If I fall asleep and noon creeps around, leave quietly and do not touch the heaters.

SARAH   Yes, sir.

SARAH goes back to her bill paying.

BIDDLE   If I fall asleep, perhaps you could type the Furukawa letter at home?

SARAH   Yes, sir. And, sir, if you'll trust me to sign the letter, I can take the manuscript to the Post Office before I come in, in the morning.

BIDDLE   Are you suggesting that you'd forge my signature?

SARAH   No, no, no. The custom is to sign it with my signature and then, under it, to write "as per Judge Biddle." Professor Furukawa would know that your secretary signed it, with your permission.

BIDDLE   That's just rude. It's not my custom and you don't have my permission.

SARAH   All right, sir. I'll bring it in and I'll go to the Post Office after you've signed it.

BIDDLE   You're saving all the postal receipts, aren't you?

SARAH   Yes, sir.

BIDDLE   Deductible, you know.

SARAH   Yes, sir.

BIDDLE   *(after a pause)* Sarah?

SARAH   *(going to his cot)* Yes, sir?

BIDDLE   I assume you've got good medical coverage for prenatal care and all that?

SARAH   Thankfully, yes.

BIDDLE   Good.

> *BIDDLE reaches down, to pull up the afghan. SARAH helps cover him.*

Sarah?

SARAH   Yes, sir?

BIDDLE   There may be a solution to your situation, or there may not. But you must have this child, and treasure it.

SARAH   Yes, sir. I'm certainly going to try.

> *Blackout.*

ACT TWO

SCENE TWO

*Friday morning, mid-April, 1968. Because BIDDLE
rarely goes to his desk now, his cot has been moved
close to SARAH's desk. As the lights come up, we
hear BIDDLE coming up the stairs. He ascends
more arduously than he did at the opening of the
play.*

*When he enters the room he wears a cap and a light
raincoat. He is winded. He pauses and looks at the
hanger. He knows that he is too weak to stand at the
hanger. This knowledge defeats him. He goes
directly to his cot and sits on it.*

*We hear SARAH running up the stairs. BIDDLE
reaches up and removes his cap. SARAH enters,
wearing a spring coat, carrying the coffee tray, the
mail, and the envelope of letters she typed at home.
She works frequently now at BIDDLE's desk, and is
quite at home there. When BIDDLE speaks, his
speech is slightly more laboured than before.*

SARAH   Good morning.

BIDDLE   Morning. Thank God it's Friday.

*SARAH deposits the tray and the mail and then
hangs up her coat. She is five months' pregnant and
is beginning to "show." She wears a loose dress
with an "empire" bodice.*

SARAH   (*scolding him*) You are not supposed to be here this
early.

BIDDLE   Madam, do not take that tone with me. You're not
supposed to be this late.

SARAH   I'm sorry, I stopped for a little chat with Mrs. Biddle. How about some coffee, to warm you up?

BIDDLE How about not right now.

A moment passes as SARAH moves about the set.

SARAH   Nice to see the tulips and daffies up.

BIDDLE Yes. Cook's got a big pot of crocus on the kitchen windowsill. Katherine and I were in Holland once, at tulip time. Most astonishing display I've ever seen.

SARAH goes to the first heater, crouches, and turns it on.

SARAH   It must have been.

Pause.

Did Doctor Wellington actually come to the house?

BIDDLE Yep. House call. Four-star-fish-and-loaves-miracle. The nice thing about a house call is they don't leave you waiting on some table, buck-naked.

SARAH   What did he say?

BIDDLE Said it would pass. As will life, I told him.

SARAH goes to the second heater, crouches, and turns it on.

We were in London, too, years ago, at lilac time. "Go down to Kew in lilac time, in lilac time, in lilac time—"

SARAH   "Go down to Kew in lilac time, it isn't far from London."

BIDDLE   All good Canadians know that.

SARAH   All good Canadians worth their salt.

BIDDLE   Did you have lilacs in Saskatoon?

SARAH   Oh, yes. Lilacs, followed by peonies.

> *He sees her going to his desk.*

BIDDLE   Come help me.

SARAH   No, sir. Not 'till it's warmer in here.

BIDDLE   *(sighing deeply)* Very well. Whatever you say.

> *She is now familiar with everything on BIDDLE's desk. She rifles through some papers to find a specific letter of inquiry.*

Tell me about spring on the prairie.

SARAH   Well, you can't talk about spring on the prairie unless you talk about winter on the prairie. A full week of forty below wasn't unusual.

BIDDLE   Mmmm. That dry, piercing cold.

SARAH   *(taking the mail out of the sack)* Glacial cold. Actually, Saskatoon is on the same latitude as Moscow. So spring is about one thing: the thaw. The Saskatchewan river runs through Saskatoon, and in March everyone in the city lays down bets as to when the "ice will go out." They try to guess the exact day that the ice will break up and the big, ten-foot-thick slabs will start to rumble and move, and pile up against the bridges.

BIDDLE   Sounds very dramatic.

SARAH   Oh, it is. In 1905 the ice took one of the bridges out
            with it! And then, almost immediately, all the back-
            yard rinks melt, and the loons come back to the lakes,
            and the farmers ready the ploughs. And on the
            outskirts of the city there's mile after mile of wild cro-
            cus. Not like Cook's potted purple ones. Not domesti-
            cated. Pale mauve, and fuzzy, and very perfumed. We
            used to gather them up and carry them home in our
            dirndl skirts.

BIDDLE   A far, far cry from Georgetown.

SARAH   Oh, my, yes.

BIDDLE   But indelible in the mind.

SARAH   *(in nostalgic agreement)* Indelible.

BIDDLE   It's warm now, come help me.

SARAH   No, sir, I can still feel the damp. *(holding the letter of
            inquiry)* Let me make one, quick call. *(sitting at his
            desk)*

BIDDLE   Woe is me. You're a hard-hearted Hannah. And may
            I say, now that you've taken control of my desk, you
            needn't relish the victory quite so much.

SARAH   You're being paranoid.

BIDDLE   You should see yourself. You look downright
            territorial.

SARAH   Bosh and bunkum.

BIDDLE   You do. *Seigniorial*, as the French say. Like a feudal
            lord. Or perhaps, more appropriate to your ancestry,
            like a laird of the fiefdom.

> *She opens her dictation book at a certain place. She dials the phone.*

SARAH   Hello, is this Mr. Joshua Crockett? This is Sarah Schorr in Judge Biddle's office. You're welcome. Yes, I think I have the information you need. May I read it from my dictation? On your first question: *(reading)* They sailed for Nuremburg on the *Queen Elizabeth.* Judge Biddle said the ship was still shabby from carrying troops. On your second question, about the American Tribunal, Justice Robert Jackson, who had of course taken leave from the bench, and Judge Biddle, and their five assistants, were housed together at Number Two, Hebelstrasse.

> *BIDDLE corrects her pronunciation.*

BIDDLE   Hebelstrasse.

SARAH   Hebelstrasse. Third question: Rudolph Hess attempted suicide twice. A commission of neurological experts reported that he was a "psychopathic personality."

> *BIDDLE laughs. SARAH holds her hand over the phone.*

Excuse me.

(to BIDDLE) Is that wrong?

BIDDLE   *(chuckling)* No, but reporting that Hess was a psychopathic personality is rather like reporting that Hitler wasn't very well-adjusted.

SARAH   *(on the phone)* I'm sorry. On your last question, Judge Biddle says that the radio broadcasts were unquestionably treasonable. He said they indicted eleven of the worst of them and convicted five.

The five were Axis Sally, Tokyo Rose, Mr. Guess Who, Paul Revere and Joe Scanlon. They were all sent to prison. You're very welcome. I'll type this up and mail it to you.

> *Crockett asks to speak to BIDDLE. SARAH gestures at the receiver, asking BIDDLE if he will take the call. BIDDLE replies "no."*

No, I'm sorry, he's unable to take calls today. Yes, I will. Thank you. Goodbye.

> *She hangs up.*

He says to be sure to thank you.

> *She goes to BIDDLE at the cot.*

> *During the following, she helps him stand, to remove his coat. Afterward, she helps him sit again. She then takes the hat and coat to the bentwood hanger.*

BIDDLE Did you see the cover of *LIFE* Magazine?

SARAH Yes. Mrs. King and the children.

BIDDLE Nixon, Humphrey, Kennedy, McCarthy—whole kit and caboodle went to the funeral.

SARAH I didn't realize he was only thirty-nine.

BIDDLE Do you know any Black people? I mean, anyone who would actually talk to you about the assassination?

SARAH No, I don't.

BIDDLE Neither do I. Therein lies the root of the problem. We don't live with them, we don't go to school with them, we don't work with them. One of their poets,

Zora Neale Hurston, said, "You can't know there 'till you go there."

SARAH Did you hear Bobby Kennedy's eulogy?

BIDDLE I did. Rather naive, though, to think he could quell their rage by saying that a white man assassinated his brother.

> *Brief pause.*

Katherine met Zora once. Some kind of poetry salon. New York City, 1928, I think.

> *SARAH is hanging up his coat. He tries to lift his legs onto the cot. He is unable to raise them. He groans, in disgust.*

SARAH Wait a minute. *(sternly)* I wish you would just wait for me.

> *Gently, she lifts his legs onto the cot. She props pillows behind him, so that he can sit.*

BIDDLE I'm always waiting for you. I start the damn day waiting for you. And if you take that tone with me one more time you're going to find yourself smack back at the employment agency.

SARAH Yes, yes, yes.

> *SARAH now places the "secretary's chair" next to the cot. BIDDLE knows what's coming.*

BIDDLE Oh, God, no. Must we?

SARAH We must.

> *She goes to a drawer in her desk and finds a tube of Ben Gay. She takes it to the cot, and sits in her chair.*

BIDDLE   I hate the damn smell.

SARAH   But you love the relief.

BIDDLE   *(in a sarcastic sing-song)* Just as Granny did.

SARAH   Just as Granny did.

> *A moment passes in silence. She massages his left hand, very gently, with the ointment. They both begin to relax into this now familiar routine.*

BIDDLE   More bad news about great-nephew Michael. Word has it that he got on a Greyhound bus and he's "crashing" somewhere in San Francisco.

SARAH   Probably Haight-Ashbury.

BIDDLE   The first sentence on the Rosetta stone, second century B.C., is "What is the matter with the next generation?"

> *A moment passes. She moves around to massage his right hand.*

There was an unusually warm, sunny day last week—

SARAH   Thursday.

BIDDLE   Maybe. Don't know anymore. Anyway, I went out for an afternoon walk. Just a short one, you know, around Thirtieth and "P." And I had a, I had a sort of a prescient moment about my mortality.

SARAH   *(suspiciously)* Your mortality.

BIDDLE   Yes.

SARAH   If this is going to be a dirge, I don't want to hear it.

BIDDLE   I don't think it is. I knew that I wouldn't die out there, but somehow I knew that it would be my last afternoon walk. So I looked down at the sidewalk and I realized it was time to say goodbye.

SARAH   Surely not to the sidewalk?

BIDDLE   No, no, no.

        Pause.

To my shadow.

        SARAH takes this in slowly. She is on the brink of tears.

SARAH   Oh, sir.

BIDDLE   *(shaking a finger at her)* Don't you dare!

SARAH   No, sir, I won't. I'll just go and wash my hands.

        She rises, puts the Ben Gay back in the drawer, and goes to the bathroom.

BIDDLE   If I hear anything resembling tears, I will rise like a phoenix and go right through this ceiling.

SARAH   All you will hear is the water running.

BIDDLE   I'm awfully glad you're done with your morning upchuck.

SARAH   So am I.
        (as she enters) Please don't talk to me while the water's running because I won't be able to hear you.

BIDDLE   Are you feeling anything yet?

SARAH   *(smiling)* Yes, last week. *(touching her stomach)* A couple of kicks.

> *She leaves the bathroom door open and we see her at the sink. We hear the water running.*

BIDDLE   Sarah?

SARAH   *(shouting back, impatiently)* Yes?

BIDDLE   I want to add something to the Groton section.

SARAH   Wait a minute!

BIDDLE   *(mumbling to himself)* All I do is wait.

> *She re-enters and goes to her desk.*

SARAH   What did you say?

BIDDLE   I want to add something to the Groton section. I can't sit at the dictaphone today. Get your book.

> *She finds her steno book.*

SARAH   I think the Groton section is fascinating.

BIDDLE   Do you mean that, or are you apple polishing?

SARAH   Sir, I don't apple polish.

BIDDLE   No, you don't. A quality that is sometimes a blessing and sometimes a curse.

SARAH   *(reacting with good humour)* Where will this be placed?

BIDDLE   Somewhere around the little blue suits with the Eton collars. *(dictating)* "We were forbidden, on Sunday, to do anything but write our parents."

>*Feelings of desolation that go back seventy-five years overwhelm him.*

Our parents.

SARAH   *(quietly)* Would you like to do this later?

BIDDLE   No, no, no, I want to do it now.

(He begins again.) "We were forbidden, on Sunday, to do anything but write our parents. No skating on the pond, no sports, certainly no cards. And there was terrific, brutal punishment from the upper forms if you stepped out of line. The Reverend Endicott Peabody reminded us, *ad nauseam*, that, 'His strength is as the strength of ten because his heart is pure.' But I had no strength at all, and the impurest of hearts— all of this manifested by a photograph, hidden deeply in my dresser drawer—"

(He smiles at the memory.) "A photograph of a 'pin-up'—surely one of the first pin-ups ever, a photo of a naughty, gorgeous young girl."

(to SARAH) That last bit ran-on terribly. Will you fix it?

SARAH   Yes, I will.

BIDDLE   *(dictating)* "Her name was Evelyn Nesbit. She was my secret for a brief interval, but by the time I graduated she was known on Broadway as 'The Girl in the Red Velvet Swing'".

>*He enjoys this memory for a moment.*

Slip it in there appropriately, will you?

SARAH   Yes, sir.

> *The house phone buzzes. SARAH answers.*

Yes, Mrs. Biddle.

> *Katherine says:"Have you broached it yet?"*

No, Ma'am. Not yet.

> *Katherine says: "Do you think you can today?"*

Yes, I will. Very soon.

> *Katherine says: "I'm sorry to bother you, but I'm so anxious."*

Understandably.

> *Katherine says: "Thank you, Sarah."*

You're welcome.

> *SARAH hangs up.*

BIDDLE   Katherine?

SARAH   Yes.

BIDDLE   What did she want?

SARAH   *(with a sudden gravity)* Sir, I have to talk to you about something.

> *She sits in the "secretary's chair," which is still alongside the cot.*

BIDDLE   Heavens, look at the brow! Furrowed with the weight of the world.

SARAH   Sir, Mrs. Biddle called me at home last night and
             asked me to come in early today for a meeting. She
             feels, and I agree, that this should be your last week,
             here in the office.

                    She awaits a reply. There is none.

             When you get here, you're no longer able to go to
             your desk. So it makes no sense to have you
             struggling across the yard, and climbing the stairs,
             just to lie on the cot.

                    *He is trying to absorb the full finality of his being
                    in this room.*

             We'll take the dictaphone to the house, and then if
             you find that you need to urgently dictate—

BIDDLE   *(barely audible)* "Need to dictate urgently."

SARAH   If you need to dictate urgently, you can do it there.
             Then I will bring the dictaphone here, and do the
             transcription, and bring the letters to the house, for
             signature. I'll continue to work here, and if you need
             anything, all you'll have to do is buzz me on the
             phone.

BIDDLE   *(very quietly)* You'd think a spouse of fifty years
             would not have to delegate this matter.

SARAH   Sir, she has alluded to it many times and you
             wouldn't discuss it. And she was afraid of a tune-up.
             Mrs. Biddle is rather frail herself these days. She
             asked my opinion and I—

BIDDLE   *(holding up his hand)* Do you mind? Please go and get
             my *vitae.* I want it to be accurate for the press.

                    SARAH goes to a file and finds his curriculum
                    vitae.

Do you know where it is?

SARAH   Yes, I've seen the file in passing.

BIDDLE   The secretary who typed it is the same damn one that started the fire. The woman's ineptitude was catastrophic.

SARAH   *(tongue in cheek)* I know, sir, but isn't that a surprising contradiction?

BIDDLE   What do you mean?

SARAH   That she was such a catastrophe even though her shorthand was Gregg?

BIDDLE   *(feigning displeasure)* Madam, you are bold.

SARAH   I'm sorry.

BIDDLE   You are not discreet.

SARAH carries the vitae *toward him.*

Read it to me.

She sits at her desk and reads.

SARAH   A.B., Harvard University, 1909. LL—

BIDDLE   *Cum laude—*

SARAH   *(writing in* cum laude*) Cum laude—*

LL.B., Harvard Law School, 1911. Person—

BIDDLE   *Cum laude—*

Again, she writes it in.

SARAH   Personal secretary, Justice Oliver Wendell Holmes, Supreme Court, 1911-1912.

BIDDLE   Let's get to the heart of the matter. Take this down, please.

> *SARAH gets her book.*

"Biddle was born and raised a Republican. It was during the Great Depression, in the nineteen-thirties, that he became acutely aware of the plight of the Pennsylvania coal miners. That is when he became a Democrat."

> *To SARAH.*

That is when I began to understand the real cost, the exhorbitant cost, the inexcusable cost, of ignoring poverty in our midst.

> *Pause.*

What's she got for 1940?

> *SARAH continues reading the* vitae.

SARAH   Solicitor General, 1940, Attorney General, 1941-45, Chief American Judge of the International Military Tribunal, Nuremberg Trials, 1945-46, Chairman, Americans for Democratic Action, 1950-53.

BIDDLE   And through it all, at every juncture, I had a running dialogue. With my absent father. What, precisely, did I say at the beginning of the Groton addition?

> *SARAH looks through her dictation book and reads:*

SARAH   "We were forbidden, on Sunday, to do anything but write our parents. No skating on—"

BIDDLE   I didn't have parents. My father died when I was six years old.

SARAH   *(holding her pen)* Do you want me to include this?

BIDDLE   No, I don't. Don't want to have a lot of maudlin blubbering on the printed page.

> *Brief pause.*

I barely remember him. His death was like some vile medicine I had to take, some noxious potion that, once swallowed, would never leave my system.

> *There is a pause. He sits upright and tries to move his legs off the cot.*

I think I'd like to go to the house now.

SARAH   Now, sir? *(checking her watch)* It's only—

BIDDLE   Please get my things.

> *SARAH goes to the hanger.*

I have very little strength, and what I have is precious.

> *During the following, SARAH gives him his cap, then helps him up and assists with his coat.*

SARAH   Did your mother re-marry?

BIDDLE   No. With four boys, she appeared to be occupied, but mostly she waited to die. I showed you her picture, didn't I?

SARAH   No, sir.

BIDDLE   *(nodding at his desk)* In my desk. Second drawer on the right.

> *He is standing as SARAH goes to get the photograph.*

And then, of course, in 1930, Katherine and I lost a son. When people who would have loved you fall out of your life, it's an indescribable sorrow. A kind of nameless pain, and nowhere in the world is there a privilege, or a promotion, or a prize that can fill the void.

> *Seeing SARAH with the photograph.*

She was beautiful, wasn't she?

SARAH   Yes, she has lovely eyes.

BIDDLE   That was before she was widowed.

> *Pause. He quotes.*

"One's eyes are what one is, one's mouth, what one becomes." John Galsworthy. May I have it, please? I'll take it to the house.

> *He puts the photograph in his coat pocket and starts for the door.*

Deterioration, debilitation, death. What an absurd plan. Isn't it strange? I've never been a slow learner, but I've only recently fully realized that when we're born, we're just visiting the world for a little while.

SARAH   Sir, would you let me help you down?

BIDDLE   No, no, no. I'll hold the rail. Go perch yourself at my desk and open the mail. "Chatelaine of a new domain."

SARAH   All right.

She moves to his desk.

BIDDLE   "Master of all you survey." "Colossus, bestriding this narrow world."

He proceeds to the door, and opens it.

Do you have a favourite title?

SARAH   I'm sorry, I don't understand.

BIDDLE   Book title. Of all the books you've read, do you have a favourite title?

SARAH   Well, I like Edmund Wilson's *Axel's Castle*. I like the way it sort of gnashes itself at you. And there's a Canadian novel called, *By Grand Central Station I Sat Down and Wept*. I've always liked that.

Pause.

What's your favourite title?

BIDDLE   It's from Vita Sackville-West. You know? Virginia Woolf's intimate friend. Not a great book, but a great title.

Pause.

All Passion Spent.

He starts out, then stops.

My mother said that people were attracted to my dad. She said he had a large circle of friends. Apparently he often had lunch with old Mrs. Gillespie. Benjamin Franklin's great-granddaughter.

Pause.

Have a good weekend.

SARAH   Thank you.

His eyes roam the room, slowly.

BIDDLE   I'll see you on Monday, at the house.

SARAH   Yes, sir.

He closes the door. SARAH, with the letter opener, opens a letter. We hear BIDDLE's halting descent.

Blackout.

ACT TWO

SCENE THREE

It is 9.30 A.M. in the third week of June, 1968.
Note: Robert Kennedy was assassinated on June 6.

As the curtain rises we see four or five opened card-
board boxes sitting around the set. These are "book"
boxes, large enough to hold books and files. One or
two might be up on tables or cabinets. BIDDLE's
desk, and other surfaces, hold stacked file folders,
many of which are fifty years old, some of which are
scorched from the fire. The dictaphone is now placed
differently from its placement in Act II, Scene I.

We can assume that BIDDLE died five days ago,
and that SARAH has worked here for two days,
since his death.

We hear SARAH coming up the stairs. She is eight
months' pregnant, "large with child," and she
mounts the stairs slowly. When she enters, she
carries the mailbag and her handbag. After placing
these items, the "house" phone buzzes. She walks,
in a lumbering manner, to the phone.

SARAH   Yes, Mrs. Biddle, good morning.

Mrs. Biddle says some semblance of "I'm very, very
worried that you're overdoing it."

Oh, please, don't worry. I promise, I won't lift anything heavy. I'll put the files in the boxes and Pierre
will tape them and carry them down.

Longer pause.

Well, Judge Biddle's lawyer suggested that I focus on three categories. Personal papers for Georgetown University, Biddle family papers for the Biddle Law Library at the University of Pennsylvania, and Nuremberg papers for Syracuse.

> *The "outside line" phone rings.*

I'm sorry, that's the outside line. 'Bye.

> *She pushes the "outside" button.*

Hello? May I ask who is calling? No, I'm sorry, Mrs. Biddle isn't taking calls today. I'm Judge Biddle's secretary, Sarah Schorr. Perhaps I can help you? Yes, Sarah with an "h". Yes, the funeral was private but there will be a memorial service at the National Cathedral at a date to be announced. No, he wasn't at home, he was at the hospital. You're welcome. Goodbye.

> *She hangs up. She lugs the "secretary's chair" over to a filing cabinet. She pulls open a drawer and stacks tattered files on the seat of the chair. She lugs the chair over to an opened box, on the cot. She lifts a handful of files. There is a faint odor of smoke in this batch. She lifts it and smells it.*

(smiling) Couldn't get it through her thick skull.

> *She puts a handful of files in the box. The phone buzzes. She lumbers over.*

Yes, Mrs. Biddle?

> *Pause.*

No, I haven't checked it yet. Do you think there's anything on it?

Pause.

He did? To whom?

Pause.

Would that be his great-great-nephew?

Pause.

Certainly, I'll check right now. I'll let you know.

> *She hangs up. She goes to the dictaphone and plugs it into a socket. She rewinds it, and starts it. We hear BIDDLE's weak voice.*

BIDDLE (*on tape*) Sarah, this is to Billy Biddle in Philadelphia. "Billy, dear boy, your letter says that you were laying in the street when you fell off your bicycle. I'm sorry that it falls to me to correct you, and I do wonder what they're teaching you at that modern boarding school."

> *Pause.*

New paragraph. "Billy, you were lying in the street, not laying. One lays only when something in one's hands needs to be laid down. 'I will lay down my book and then I will lie on my bed.' I hope you're not offended, and I know you think me an old curmudgeon, but, you see, our language is deteriorating at the speed of light. Regards to your parents, good luck on the finals, Love, etcetera."

> *SARAH waits a moment to see if there is more. Just as she is about to stop the tape, she hears:*

Sarah? I doubt that I'll see you again. I want you to know that I applaud your journey thus far, my dear. Lace the skates, and hit the ice, and stay the course.

She lets the tape run a moment, until she knows there is nothing more. She pushes the stop button, then straightens her posture and puts her hands on her back.

CURTAIN

SPEAK, MEMORY
by Joanna McClelland Glass

In the autumn of 1967, in Washington, D.C., I began work as a secretary to Francis Biddle. He was 81 at the time. He had been Attorney General under Franklin Roosevelt, 1941-1945. In 1946, Harry Truman appointed him to be Chief American Judge of the International Military Tribunal at the Nuremberg Trials. On my first day of employment he told me, quite emphatically, that he was certain he was in his final year of life. He died in October of 1968.

Judge Biddle was a "Main Line Philadelphia" Biddle, a man whose family came to the colonies from England in 1681. Upon arriving, his first American ancestor, William Biddle, purchased 43,000 acres of what is now New Jersey from William Penn. I was a green young girl from the Canadian prairie. My native city, Saskatoon, Saskatchewan, was incorporated in 1906. In 1906 the young Francis Biddle was an undergraduate at Harvard, soon to enter Harvard Law. We spent our months together "trying" to negotiate and span our enormous differences of youth and age, of class and culture.

We worked in an office that was located atop a garage, an aerie that had once been a hayloft. The garage was approximately 150 feet across the yard from the Judge and Mrs. Biddle's Georgetown house. The trek from the house to the garage was a chore for him; the ensuing climb of a dozen stairs left him winded. And although his physical discomfort angered him, he reserved his deepest rage for the way in which his once-brilliant mind now betrayed him. He fluctuated between "lucidity and senility," as he says in my play. Occasionally he confused me with a secretary who had started a fire in the office after leaving the gas heaters on. Always a vigilant grammarian, occasionally he resorted to tirades against my use of split infinitives. Occasionally he drove me to tears, but I knew that I was witnessing a man of great intellectual stature doing battle, fiercely, with his mortality. And as our sometimes comical, sometimes argumentative days together passed, my fondness for him grew.

My first awkward stab at playwriting was *Santacqua*, produced in December of 1969 at Herbert Berghof's Playwright's Unit on Bank Street in Greenwich Village. A year later I wrote the first version of *Trying*, in the form of a one-act play. I sent it to Herbert, requesting an opinion. He replied enthusiastically and insisted that I send the play to his old friend, Alfred Lunt. And so it happened, in April of 1971, that the then 78-year-old actor called me from "Ten Chimneys," his Wisconsin farm. It was an unusually warm spring day in Detroit. I was mixing a pitcher of Kool-Aid and was surrounded by, and overwhelmed by, my three noisy children when the phone rang. (I had three kids in two years, due to twins.) Mr. Lunt said that he found the contradictions in Biddle—the "radical patrician" aspects of him—fascinating, and went on to say that he would very much like to play the part. And then, sadly, he said, "But I'm afraid I can't play anymore because I'm going blind, and I bump into things." I put the play away but the image of Biddle fending off the Grim Reaper lingered with me across almost four decades.

Four years ago I returned to the material to write a full-length play. I struggled with many drafts because it seemed, at first, that the only appropriate "homage" would be to depict the man at the height of his powers. To portray him arguing with Henry Stimson, Secretary of War, in Roosevelt's Cabinet, or in a German courtroom confronting Goering or Hess or Speer or Ribbentrop. But all attempts at historical biography ran aground on the shoals of "research." That is, I could not make information lifted from Biddle's own, autobiographical accounts, work on the stage. It resisted fluid dramatization. Every attempt lacked the ring of truth; every attempt had about it a dull aura of removed, lifted information.

Finally, I went back to the 45-minute one-act play and found that I had recorded there what I consider to be the essentials of the Judge's final year. He was, much of the time, utterly frustrated with the naiveté of my youthful convictions and pronouncements. He was frequently in a state of aggravation over articles, journals and files that had been destroyed in the fire. He was obsessed with the two deaths that forever changed his life. (His father had died when Judge Biddle was only six years old, and one of his sons, Garrison Chapin Biddle, had died when only seven years old.) And he deeply regretted, in his mind, his heart and all of his written correspondence, his role as Attorney General during the internment of 125,000 Japanese-American citizens during World War II. It is on these basic essentials that I strove to construct the full-length, two-hour play.

JOANNA MCCLELLAND GLASS was born in Saskatoon, Saskatchewan. Her plays have been produced in many North American regional theatres, as well as in England, Ireland, Australia, and Germany.

Her one-act plays, *Canadian Gothic* and *American Modern*, were first produced at the Manhattan Theatre Club in New York City in 1972. *Artichoke*, starring Colleen Dewhurst, was first produced at Long Wharf Theatre, New Haven, CT, in 1974. *To Grandmother's House We Go*, starring Eva LeGallienne, was first produced at the Alley Theatre, Houston, Texas, moving to Broadway in 1980. *Play Memory*, directed by Harold Prince, was first produced at the McCarter Theatre, Princeton, New Jersey, moving to Broadway in 1984. *Play Memory* won a Tony Award nomination that year. *Yesteryear* was originally produced by Canadian Stage Company in Toronto in 1989, and was selected to open the 1998 summer season of the Blyth Festival. *If We Are Women* premiered in the U.S. in the summer of 1993, at the Williamstown Theatre Festival, Williamstown, MA. The Canadian premiere was a co-production between the Vancouver Playhouse and Canadian Stage Company, Toronto, 1994. The British premiere was in London, starring Joan Plowright, directed by Richard Olivier.

Trying was first produced by Victory Gardens Theatre in Chicago in the spring of 2004. The same production moved to The Promenade Theatre in New York City, in the fall of 2004.

Ms. Glass has written two novels, *Reflections of a Mountain Summer* published by Alfred A. Knopf in 1975, and *Woman Wanted* published by St. Martin's Press in 1984. She has adapted both novels into screenplays. *Woman Wanted* was filmed in 1998, starring and directed by Kiefer Sutherland, also starring Holly Hunter and Michael Moriarty.

In 1984-85, Ms. Glass was awarded a Rockefeller grant. She was playwright-in-residence that year at Yale Repertory Theatre, New Haven, CT. Other grants: the National Endowment for the Arts, 1980, the Guggenheim Fellowship in 1981, the Francesca Primus Award in 1994 and the Berrilla Kerr Award in 2000.